Anger Management
Friendship
School Success
Self-Concept

SMALL GROUP
Counseling

FOR CHILDREN

By Diane S. Senn, Ed.S.

Cover Design by Elaine Callahan
Layout/graphics by Elaine Callahan
Project Supervisor - Susan Bowman
Project Editing - Susan Bowman

ISBN 1-889636-54-1

Library of Congress
2003101944

10 9 8 7 6 5 4 3 2
Printed in the United States of America

P.O. Box 115
Chapin, South Carolina 29036
(800) 209-9774 • (803) 345-1070
Fax (803) 345-0888 • Email YL@sc.rr.com
www.youthlight.com

TABLE OF CONTENTS

Dedication

To all the caring adults who give of
their heart, their hands, their head, and their time
to help our children grow to be healthy, happy adults.

Acknowledgments

I would like to thank the following people for their contributions to this book:

To my friend and fellow counselor, Gwen Sitsch, who supported, encouraged and gave of her time to review, share feedback, and edit each page of the book..

To Betts Gatewood for her time and effort in reading and editing...and for her continued friendship and support.

To Bob and Susan Bowman for their willingness in supporting, encouraging, promoting, reviewing, editing, and for their belief in this project.

To Elaine Callahan for her creativity in formatting and including graphics to bring 'life' to the pages.

To my children, Bryan and Lindsay, and to my husband Stan for their unconditional love, support, and their faith in me that I could accomplish this task.

And most importantly we give honor and thanks to God, our guiding light.

Introduction

What small group topics are covered in this book?

ANGER MANAGEMENT	FRIENDSHIP
SCHOOL SUCCESS SKILLS	SELF CONCEPT

What's in the book?

- **Newsletter information about groups**
- **Small group reminder notices**
- **Small group roster and planning form**
- **Service learning activities**
- **Pre and post assessments**
- **Teacher notes & parent letters**
- **Feedback forms**
- **Step by step directions for setting up the group**
- **Icebreakers/energizer activities**
- **Skill building activities**

What's UNIQUE about this book?

- Choices of activities are provided for you to design your own group that relates to your groups' specific needs. Both icebreaker/energizer activities as well as main topic activities are given as choices.
- Needs assessment activities are provided for each group topic to help determine the specific areas of need for group participants. A correlation chart correlating the needs with the skill building activities is given for each group topic.
- A small group roster and planning form is given that includes a space for listing of group members, attendance roll with related needs, a planning outline for the different components of each session, and an area for recording observations/notes from each group meeting.
- Post assessment activities are provided for each group topic to determine the success of the group.
- Includes parent/teacher information on various skill building activities enlisting their help to reinforce the targeted skill.
- Includes a brief 5-10 minute Service Learning Component that can be added to each group session. Service Learning has multiple benefits to the recipient and to the doer of the good deed.

For more information on how to use this book keep reading...

The Purpose of this book is...

The main emphasis of this book is to provide a variety of activities and brief lessons to stimulate interaction and learning on the various topics. Information on four main group topics is included– Anger Management, Friendship, School Success Skills, and Self Concept. The unique part of this book is that it is set up as a resource for you to choose which activities will best meet the needs of your particular group. As you know, each group of students is different with different needs. From my own experience when I have set up a group, for example on friendship, the needs go anywhere from overcoming shyness and learning to meet people to overbearing, bossy behavior that causes problems in friendships. Clearly having only one predetermined six session group activities on friendship may not meet the specific needs of the group. Therefore this book offers a variety of activities that you can choose from depending on the need. To assist in determining the needs a Needs Assessment Activity is provided for each of the group topics. The needs assessment includes gathering information from the students, the teacher, and the parents and then correlating those needs to specific activities using the correlation chart given for each group. From there a Small Group Roster and Planning Form is included to write down the activities you are planning for the group based on the needs. On this form there is also a place to add observations and notes to keep in mind for the next meeting. The roster is on page 21. To conclude the group a final activity is provided that includes a post assessment from the student, teacher, and parent.

Background information about small groups...

Benefits and Cautions of Small Group Counseling

Small group counseling is a vital part of the Developmental Guidance and Counseling program. In his book, *Group Counseling A Developmental Approach,* Gazda summarized groups as a preventive, growth-engendering, and remedial process. Groups have the flexibility of reinforcing appropriate skills for normal developmental problems, they can provide help at the first signs of difficulty in coping with a situation, and groups can give support and skill enhancement for more difficult situations. Myrick in his *Developmental Guidance and Counseling: A Practical Approach,* presented the following advantages and limitations of small group counseling. Advantages and benefits of small group counseling are summarized as follows:

- Small groups provide an avenue of reaching and helping more students in a timely, efficient manner.
- Students learn from each other. Students can offer support and encouragement.
- Many problems that people experience are related to social interaction therefore small groups provide that social arena in which to observe and practice behaviors and feelings related to the problem.
- The sense of belonging and togetherness in group counseling creates a unique learning climate.
- Group members can practice behaviors, receive feedback and suggestions from others. Peer feelings and ideas often have more credibility than those of adults.
- As group members facilitate one another, the counselor has more time to reflect on what a person is saying, how they are responding, and some possible alternatives.
- Instead of the counselor being the only resource for a student the group members provide an additional resource.
- Some students find it too intense to meet with an adult alone. The presence of peers helps reduce the tension and the feeling of being singled out for counseling.

Small groups provide the opportunity for students to express themselves and be heard, the opportunity for students to show concern for others and sense concern from others, and the chance to realize that others have similar problems or concerns.

Some limitations or cautions of small group counseling are:

- Small group counseling may not be the most effective strategy for every situation or every person.
- It can be more challenging to establish trust and close working relationships when there are more people and behaviors to work together with.
- The small group counseling process is more complex since there are more variables to which the counselor needs to attend.
- It takes more energy and time to coordinate and facilitate a small group as opposed to meeting with an individual.
- Confidentiality is more difficult to safeguard, as more people share in the communication.
- Some issues appear too sensitive, too emotional, and too complex to work with in a group.

Small group counseling can provide overwhelming positive effects but it is our job as counselors to assess situations and to organize and structure groups being aware of the group cautions so that we can ensure success for the group counseling that is offered.

Leadership Skills

One of the most important ingredients in successful small group counseling is the counselor's leadership skills. It is the leader's responsibility to structure, connect, model, involve everyone and to be able to 'read' a situation to determine the best direction of the group. The first step to good leadership skills is the knowledge of what the particular leadership skills are. The next step is to be able to effectively implement these skills in an ever changing group. Leadership skill success takes knowledge and practice. The following is a list of the basic leadership skills.

1. Structuring
2. Modeling
3. Promoting Group Equality and Cohesiveness
4. Connecting (Linking)
5. Paraphrasing and Clarifying
6. Redirecting
7. Summarizing

Check additional resources for more information about small group leadership skills, group stages, and ethical standards in conducting small groups. As professionals we have a responsibility to remain knowledgeable about our ethical standards in small group counseling as well as the best practices in leading small groups.

Just some thoughts...

Group size can vary anywhere from three to eight students. Consider the age of the student – the younger the student the fewer the students. Consider the topic of the small group – if it is an intense topic where more attention will be needed for each student smaller groups are preferred. Consider the behavior and needs of the students – the more difficult to manage student and increased student needs require a smaller number in the group.

What is the length and duration of the group? Groups typically meet for thirty to forty- five minutes each session for six to eight sessions. You need a minimum of six meetings in order to allow time for group cohesiveness and to reach the working stage; however, additional sessions may be added.

How do you find a scheduled time for group? There are many ways to set up and schedule groups with teachers. When there is a specific need for a group, consult with the teacher for a specific day and time during the week to meet. If students change classes and teachers, you may devise a plan to rotate the group to a different time each week so they do not miss the same teacher/class each week. Or at the beginning of the year ask each grade level teacher to provide an acceptable day/time to pull students for groups during the year. Rather than the traditional meeting of once a week for six to eight weeks consider trying twice a week for three to four weeks. I find that the concentrated meeting of twice a week helps us to remain more focused and maintain better continuity.

Consider the four stages of a group: Involvement, transition, working and closure. Use your group leadership skills to develop trust and cooperation in the beginning stages of the group and to provide insight during the working stage of the group and commitment at closure.

Managing Group Behavior: Different strategies are needed for different groups. Some groups will have an automatic cohesiveness and will be ready and productive in working together. Other groups will need more time to build cohesiveness and a comfort level to be productive. Still other groups may have resistant members whose behaviors counteract the goals of the group. For these resistant groups, select activities that encourage involvement and give control to group members. In some of my younger groups where behavior was unfocused, I began handing out plastic chips to them along with a compliment about their listening or answering a question or showing support for a fellow member. I gave out chips frequently and even just tossed a chip to them and told them I saw them doing something well and asked if they knew what it was. I have been amazed at the positive response in this. At the end of group I did not give any rewards for chips earned (the reward is in the compliment and in doing the right thing). I asked them to quietly count their chips and return them to me. I went to each student and had them whisper how many they had earned at which time I again complimented them on a great job and then collected their chips. If there are obvious behavior problems with group members then behavior modification techniques may be needed to address the problem. In this case, helping the child's behavior becomes the primary or secondary goal of group. If they are acting that way in group then there is a good chance that is how they act in the classroom and other group environments. If a student still persists in disrupting the group and other positive management strategies have been tried, the student can be removed from the group. As you talk to the student about leaving the group do not present this in a punitive manner because this apparently is a student you need to really connect with and work with. Instead explain to the student that his/her behavior seems to show that perhaps this group is not the right group for him/her that he/she doesn't seem to be comfortable and wanting to be part of a group. Explain that you will be glad to look for another group for him/her to be a part of and perhaps the two of you could get together and talk and work on things until then.

Tutorial
FOR SMALL GROUP COUNSELING

12 Steps in Planning and Conducting Small Group Counseling:

Step 1: Use the Newsletter Information Regarding Small Groups (see page 11) to obtain any parent referrals for their child to participate in a small group.

Step 2: Send the Teacher Note and the Teacher Recommendation Form (see pages 12-13) to teachers to obtain any referrals from teachers.

Step 3: With the information obtained from the above forms and your own knowledge of the students select the group topic and students for group.

Step 4: Coordinate with the teacher to select a good meeting time for the small group.

Step 5: Talk with each student and invite them to be part of the group. Send home the Parent Letter Regarding Student's Participation in Small Group Counseling (see page 14) to obtain permission or agreement for their child to participate.

Step 6: Add the students' names and any related needs on the Small Group Roster and Planning Form (see pages 19-22).

Step 7: Review the Getting Started: First Group Session (see page 17). Select your icebreaker/energizer from the Icebreaker/Energizer section. Review the Needs Assessment Activity (first activity listed in each group topic section). Copy and collect any materials needed for the activity. Decide if the optional Service Learning Component will be used in the group. If so, then review the general information and the Secret Service Initial Information for Students to prepare for the first meeting (see pages 280-282).

Step 8: Follow your plans for the first meeting. Before students leave, distribute a Small Group Reminder Notice (see page 15) to each student as a reminder of future group meetings.

Step 9: After the first group meeting collect and review the Needs Assessments to determine the specific needs of the group. Use the Activities' Correlation chart found in each group topic section to determine which activities would be helpful for the group's future sessions. Complete the remainder of the Small Group Roster and Planning Form adding icebreaker/energizer activities, skill building activities, and service learning assignments if you are choosing to do that component.

Step 10: Use your counseling skills during each session to connect with students, help students connect and support each other, to provide skill building activities and a safe environment to practice these new skills as you work together at each session.

Step 11: Send a completed Small Group Feedback Form for Parents and Teachers (when appropriate) to keep them involved, helping, and working together for the student. Some parent/teacher information letters are already provided in some lessons.

Step 12: Review the How to End: Final Group Session (see page 23) and plan for the group's closure. For this last group session complete the final group activity given. Distribute and collect the students', teachers', and parents' post assessments. Review these assessments to determine successes and area of remaining weaknesses. Plan a follow up for the group members - either a monthly meeting, individual counseling, or a note to check on the student.

Step 13: (Oh well – baker's dozen) Give yourself a pat on the back for a job well done!

Forms, Notes and Outlines

Forms, Notes and Outlines
for SMALL GROUPS

Small Group
NEWSLETTER

Information for Small Group Counseling

Small group counseling is offered to students to support and enhance the development of personal and social skills and to support and promote educational success. Small groups provide not only additional social-emotional learning experiences but also allows the students a chance to belong, a chance to express themselves, and a chance to benefit from the support of group members.

Groups are offered on an "as needed" basis. Children may be referred to certain groups by parents, teachers, or themselves. While students are encouraged to share with their parents about group and what they are doing and learning, they agree to keep confidential personal information shared by other students.

Below is a list of some of the small groups offered during the year:

Anger Control – intended for students who need or would like to work on dealing and managing their angry feelings in a positive way. Group will explore the triggers of our anger and then build the skills to handle that area more effectively.

Friendship – Children need the acceptance and the support of their peers. The friendship group is intended for students who need or would like to work on strengthening their friendship skills. The group will focus on acknowledging and strengthening our friendship qualities we have to offer others, how to connect and communicate with others, building friendly behaviors and dealing with friendship problems.

School Success Skills – Being successful in school is the foundation to a student's future. School Success Skills group will explore and strengthen the skills for school success. Depending on the specific needs of the group, the group may focus on listening and attending skills, organization, study tips, homework tips, test taking tips, and attitude.

Self-Concept – Building and maintaining a positive self-concept is important in being a happy, productive person. In group we will focus on appreciating our strengths and the things we can do well, and then developing positive thoughts and skills to handle when things don't go right.

If there is a particular group from which you believe your child would benefit, please call or send a note.

TEACHER NOTE
For Recommendations For Small Group Counseling

To: Teachers

From:

Re: Small groups

Date:

Small group counseling is offered to students to support and enhance the development of personal and social skills and to support and promote educational success. Small groups provide not only additional social-emotional learning experiences but also allows the students a chance to belong, a chance to express themselves, and a chance to benefit from the support of group members.

As you get to know your students and specific needs arise, consider participation in a small counseling group to meet these specific needs. Possible topics for groups are:

Anger Control – Intended for students who need or would like to work on dealing and managing their angry feelings in a positive way. Group will explore the triggers of our anger and then build the skills to handle that area more effectively.

Friendship – Friendship group is intended for students who need or would like to work on strengthening their friendship skills. Group will focus on acknowledging and strengthening our friendship qualities we have to offer others, how to connect and communicate with others, building friendly behaviors and dealing with friendship problems.

School Success Skills – School Success Skills group will explore and strengthen the skills for school success. Depending on the specific needs of the group, the group may focus on listening and attending skills, organization, study tips, homework tips, test taking tips, and attitude.

Self-Concept – Building and maintaining a positive self-concept is important in being a happy, productive person. In group we will focus on appreciating our strengths and the things we can do well, and then developing positive thoughts and skills to handle when things don't go right.

Please review the above topics and/or create topics of your own that you feel meets the needs of your students. Complete the attached form to recommend a students' participation in group and return. Groups will be scheduled during the year to accommodate the need.

TEACHER RECOMMENDATION
For Small Group Form

Teacher's Name or Grade Level _____

Group Topic: **Anger Control Group**

Student's Name/Homeroom _____

1. _____
2. _____
3. _____
4. _____
5. _____
6. _____

Group Topic: **Friendship Group**

Student's Name/Homeroom _____

1. _____
2. _____
3. _____
4. _____
5. _____
6. _____

Group Topic: **School Success Skills Group**

Student's Name/Homeroom _____

1. _____
2. _____
3. _____
4. _____
5. _____
6. _____

Group Topic: **Self-Concept Group**

Student's Name/Homeroom _____

1. _____
2. _____
3. _____
4. _____
5. _____
6. _____

Additional small group topics needed:

Topic: Student: Homeroom:

_____   _____   _____

_____   _____   _____

_____   _____   _____

PARENT LETTER
Small Group Counseling

Dear Parent,

Our School Counseling Program at _____offers small group counseling for our students. Small groups provide not only the opportunity for additional learning experiences but also a time of sharing and a time of growing together with fellow students. Small groups give the students a chance to belong, a chance to express themselves, and a chance to benefit from the support of group members.

Your child _____ is invited to be a part of a small group. The group will

meet _____ during the school day.

The group will focus on:

_____

_____

_____

_____

_____

_____

Parent permission is requested for a student to participate in the group. Please return the bottom portion of this letter to your child's teacher. I will be happy to answer any questions you might have. You may reach me by calling the school.

Sincerely,

School Counselor

I agree that my child, _____ may participate in small group

counseling dealing with _____.

_____   _____
Date   Signature of Parent or Guardian

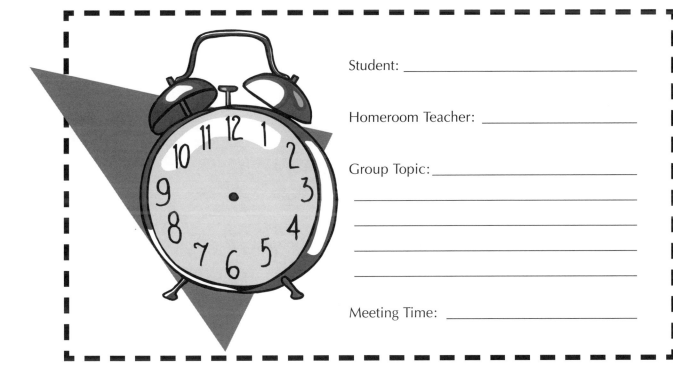

Student: _____

Homeroom Teacher: _____

Group Topic: _____

_____

_____

_____

_____

Meeting Time: _____

DON'T FORGET

To: _____

Our Small Group Meets on:

_____

_____

In the Guidance Room

See You There!

SMALL GROUP FEEDBACK FORM
For Parents and Teachers

TO: Parent/Teacher of

STUDENT: _____

GROUP:_____DATE: _____

In small group today we talked about…

_____

_____

Suggestions of ways you can reinforce this lesson…

_____

_____

TO: Parent/Teacher of

STUDENT: _____

GROUP:_____DATE: _____

In small group today we talked about…

_____

_____

Suggestions of ways you can reinforce this lesson…

_____

_____

GETTING STARTED:
First Group Session

The purpose of the first session is to establish rapport, provide a welcoming environment and help the students begin to connect with each other. The first session gives a chance to establish the framework for the group and to begin assessing group needs.

I. **GROUP PURPOSE:** Share the purpose of the group. Answer the questions: What? When? Where? and How?

II. **GROUP GUIDELINES:** The rules for small group are basically the following:
1. Take turns talking and sharing.
2. Be a good listener to others.
3. No put downs.
4. No names when sharing situations.
5. Personal information shared in group by others remains confidential.

You may share the group rules through a discussion asking the students what guidelines they think would be important for the group. Or you may choose to have the rules written on a poster to review with the group. Or you may use the following approach to share the rules:

Materials Needed:
- Picture of eyes looking or eye glasses with picture of eyes taped to the front
- Picture of an ear or a plastic ear
- Picture of a valentine heart or a heart pillow

Procedure:
1. **Introduction:** Say – *There are a few guidelines that we all need to follow in group.*
2. Put on your glasses with the eyes as you tell the group that it is important that our eyes are looking at whoever is doing the talking as we take turns sharing.
3. Hold up the ear and say that we need to be listening well to each person so that we hear what others say and can give our support.
4. Hold up the heart and say that we need to care about each other and never laugh or make fun of someone.
5. Say: *The last guideline is that personal information that group members choose to share needs to remain confidential and not shared outside the group. However you are welcome to share with your parents or others the types of things we are doing and what we may be learning in group.*

III. **ICEBREAKERS/ENERGIZERS:** Choose an activity from the Icebreakers/Energizer section.

IV. **INITIAL GROUP SESSION:** Follow the directions given for the initial activity. This activity is listed as the first activity in each small group topic section. It will direct you to complete the Student Needs Assessment and to send out and collect the Parent/Teacher Needs Assessment. After the needs assessments have been completed and returned, review and determine the main areas of need for your group. This will help you select future group activities. Use the SMALL GROUP ROSTER AND PLANNING Form to write down your plans for future group sessions.

V. **(OPTIONAL) SERVICE LEARNING COMPONENT:** If you are planning to incorporate service learning activities as part of the group, you need to introduce this to the group. Refer to the general information given at the beginning of the Service Learning Section and review the SECRET SERVICE INITIAL INFORMATION FOR STUDENTS.

SESSION PLANNING
And How To Use The Small Group Planning Form

After the initial meeting and the needs assessments have been completed and reviewed, you need to plan the future group sessions. From the various activities available, you need to select activities from the ICEBREAKERS/ENERGIZERS Section, the SMALL GROUP TOPIC Sections, and the SERVICE LEARNING Section (if you are choosing to implement this component). Turn to the table of contents in each section for an overview of activity choices. A planning sheet – **SMALL GROUP ROSTER AND PLANNING FORM** has been included to assist in the group planning. This SMALL GROUP ROSTER AND PLANNING FORM allows you to keep roll of your students attendance, homeroom teacher, and a place to add any specific needs shared by the teacher. The form also gives you a place to write out brief plans for the group in selecting the activities from the different sections – just jot down the title or the page number to refer. The plans for your group should include the following as outlined on the SMALL GROUP ROSTER AND PLANNIING FORM.

The group sessions should begin with a quick **Review** of the previous session - checking on any homework given or skills practiced. If you chose to do the Service Learning Activity this is the time for group members to report on their assignments.

Next, select an **Icebreaker/Energizer.** This selection depends on the character of the group whether they may need an active energizer, or a getting to know you activity, or simply a sharing activity. Icebreakers/Energizers are good to add but not essential for every group meeting.

Then choose the **Skill Building Activity** based on the needs of your group and implement. Some of the activities include a Parent/Teacher Note. The purpose for the notes are to engage the adult's help in encouraging and supporting the child in the new information they are learning. Notes may be sent to parents or teachers or both. You are encouraged to add a quick note of your own for those lessons that do not have one. Students need support from both home and school.

Finally assign a **Service Learning Activity** if you are including this in your group experience.

The last heading on the SMALL GROUP ROSTER AND PLANNING FORM is entitled **Observations/Notes.** This section provides a place to record any details or specifics that arise during that session that you need to remember or that need to be addressed at the next session.

Planning is important however remember to be flexible as the needs or the direction of the group may change.

Small Group Roster And Planning

Group Topic: _____

Student Name	Teacher	Sessions								Related Needs
		1	2	3	4	5	6	7	8	

SESSION 1: See Getting Started: First Group Session

Group Purpose _____

Group Guidelines_____

Icebreaker/Energizer_____

Needs Assessment Activity _____

(Optional) Service Learning Introduction _____

Observations/Notes:_____

_____

_____

SESSION 2:

Review _____

Icebreaker/Energizer_____

Skill Building Activity_____

(Optional) Service Learning Assignment _____

Observations/Notes:_____

_____

_____

SESSION 3:

Review _____

Icebreaker/Energizer_____

Skill Building Activity_____

(Optional) Service Learning Assignment _____

Observations/Notes:_____

_____

_____

SESSION 4:

Review _____

Icebreaker/Energizer _____

Skill Building Activity _____

(Optional) Service Learning Assignment _____

Observations/Notes: _____

_____

_____

SESSION 5:

Review _____

Icebreaker/Energizer _____

Skill Building Activity _____

(Optional) Service Learning Assignment _____

Observations/Notes: _____

_____

_____

SESSION 6:

Review _____

Icebreaker/Energizer _____

Skill Building Activity _____

(Optional) Service Learning Assignment _____

Observations/Notes: _____

_____

_____

SESSION 7:

Review _____

Icebreaker/Energizer _____

Skill Building Activity _____

(Optional) Service Learning Assignment _____

Observations/Notes: _____

_____

_____

SESSION 8: See How to End: Final Group Session

Observations/Notes: _____

_____

_____

PLAN FOR FOLLOW-UP: _____

_____

_____

_____

Small Group Roster And Planning

Group Topic: _Anger Management_

Student Name	Teacher	Sessions								Related Needs
		1	2	3	4	5	6	7	8	
Zach	Roberts	✓	✓							
Henry	Roberts	✓	✓							Self-Control
Savannah	Jones	✓	✓							
Jamark	Jones	✓	✓							
Shanice	Jones	✓	✓							Difficulties w/Peers
Tyler	Smith	✓	✓							

SESSION 1: See Getting Started: First Group Session

Group Purpose _Answer: What? When? Where? and How?_

Group Guidelines _p. 17 – use eyes, ears and heart pillow_

Icebreaker/Energizer _p. 29 "Cooperation Game" (Use at end of session)_

Needs Assessment Activity _Activity p. 53 "Things That Bug Me"_

(Optional) Service Learning Introduction _N/A_

Observations/Notes: _Observation from Cooperation Game: Henry demonstrated leadership skills, Shanice was frustrated easily and Tyler withdrew._
To Do: Send assessments to parents and teachers.

SESSION 2:

Review _Share results of needs assessments_

Icebreaker/Energizer _Activity p. 38 "Go Around Statements"_

Skill Building Activity _Activity A1.1 P. 59 "In Control"_

(Optional) Service Learning Assignment _Introduce (p. 280-282); Assignment P. 283_

Observations/Notes: _Encourage students to share their calming down activity sheet with their parents – provide incentives for returning it signed._

SESSION 3:

Review _Report on SL*; Review "In Control" Activity Check sheets_

Icebreaker/Energizer _N/A_

Skill Building Activity _Activity A1.3 "Positive Thinking"_

(Optional) Service Learning Assignment _Assignment p. 287_

Observations/Notes: _____

*SL – Service Learning

SESSION 4:

Review _Report on SL* Assignment; Review "Positive Thinking"_

Icebreaker/Energizer _Activity p. 36 "Freeze"_

Skill Building Activity _Activity A1.5 "The Chill Cube"_

(Optional) Service Learning Assignment _Assignment p. 292_

Observations/Notes: _____

_____

_____

SESSION 5:

Review _Report on SL* Assignment; Review "Chill Cube"_

Icebreaker/Energizer _N/A_

Skill Building Activity _Activity A2.1 "Unlocking Friendship Problems"_

(Optional) Service Learning Assignment _Assignment p. 285_

Observations/Notes: _____

_____

_____

SESSION 6:

Review _Report on SL* Assignment and Review_

Icebreaker/Energizer _Activity p. 39 "Quetions...Questions"_

Skill Building Activity _Activity A3.2 "Don't Bite the Hook"_

(Optional) Service Learning Assignment _Assignment p. 296_

Observations/Notes: _____

_____

_____

SESSION 7:

Review _Report on SL* Assignment and Review_

Icebreaker/Energizer _N/A_

Skill Building Activity _Activity A6.1 "In Trouble"_

(Optional) Service Learning Assignment _Assignment p. 297_

Observations/Notes: _____

_____

_____

SESSION 8: See How to End: Final Group Session _(p. 23) Review; Activity A10 "Anger Solutions"_

Observations/Notes: _Send Post Assessments to parents and teachers._

_____

_____

PLAN FOR FOLLOW-UP: _Meet once a month as follow-up._

_____

_____

*SL – Service Learning

HOW TO END:
Final Group Session

The purpose of the final session is to bring closure to the group, to summarize the skills discussed and to empower the student.

I. **Review:** Review the previous week's session. If students participated in the Service Learning component then have them report the results of their secret service assignment.

II. **Icebreaker:** May choose a sharing sentence such as: Share one thing that you have improved on or learned from the group.

III. **Activity:** Complete the activity listed for Final Group Session.

IV. **Evaluation:** Have students complete the post assessment form. Allow students to share information from their form if they choose. Send out and collect the Parent/Teacher Post Assessment.

V. **Group Closure:** Celebrate the group, the time together, what you like about everyone, and point out their successes. Encourage others to do the same.

VI. **Plan for Follow-Up:** Follow up with students individually, consulting with their teachers, and/or sending notes to the students to encourage and compliment. Consider scheduling a monthly support group.

Icebreakers and Energizers

Icebreakers and Energizers

Icebreakers and energizers in small groups are brief activities that are intended to bring some fun to the group, get the group moving and talking, provide a creative way for students to share, and at times provide insight into behavior and prompt further discussion.

Icebreakers and energizers are generally used at the beginning of the group meetings however they can be used at the end or even in the middle of the group if they are needed. Every group meeting does not have to have an icebreaker or energizer. There may be meetings that begin with a review of last week's session or a sharing of a homework assignment from the previous weeks' session. Or perhaps that week's main activity needs all the group time allotted. Even if you do not plan for an icebreaker or energizer for every meeting do plan for fun experience of some kind at some point during the group session.

Icebreakers and energizers are provided in this section for you to choose from to use in your groups. Your selection of the activity depends on the character and needs of the group. Some groups need an active energizer. With other groups the active energizer may get them too active and off focused. Other times you may need a getting to know you activity and other times a simple sharing activity. The selection is given to you for your choice as to what would best fit the needs of your particular group.

Use the Small Group Planning and Roster Form found in the Forms section to list the icebreakers and/or energizers you have chosen for each group meeting.

ICEBREAKER AND ENERGIZER ACTIVITIES

Cooperation Game

Purpose: A fun activity that emphasizes the importance of cooperation and allows the group leader to gain insight as to the students' group interaction skills such as: how well they get along in working together, sharing, handling frustration, taking the initiative, involving others, etc. This insight may be used in planning future group sessions. I like using this activity at the beginning of small groups.

Activity:
- **Materials Needed:** Cooperation Game Activity sheet cut apart leaving a thin outline around each piece.
- Hand each student a piece of the puzzle and explain that their goal is to put the puzzle pieces together to form one shape. Tell them that the black outline around the pieces need to face up.
- Encourage and congratulate them as they complete their task.

Discuss:
- Ask the students what they had to do in order to be successful in putting the pieces together to form one shape. Include in the discussion the importance of each person sharing their puzzle piece with the group, of sticking with it and not giving up, of gaining help and insight from another group member, and of encouraging and complimenting others to continue working.
- Check to see if you can relate any of these insights to the group topic.
- If the group had difficulty and quit or a member did not handle him/herself in an appropriate way, use your counseling skills to encourage the group to talk about what each could have done to help reach the group goal. After focusing on the positive things let them try again but perhaps this time give them a new puzzle of a circle (smiley face) – simply draw a large smiley face and cut into puzzle pieces. Compliment them and encourage them during the process. Congratulate them on their success.

Cooperation Game

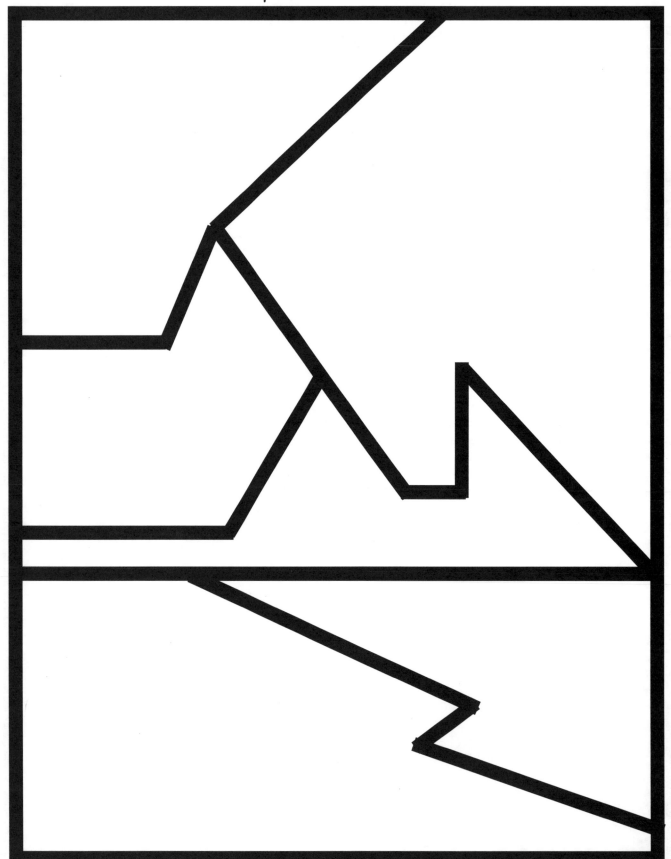

Beach Ball Fun

Purpose: An action game of sharing that involves everyone.

Activity:
- **Materials Needed:** beach ball, magic marker
- With permanent magic marker write a series of questions on the ball, one question for each segment (suggestions for questions are given below). However in one of the segments add a silly direction such as, "hop like a frog" or "crow like a rooster".
- Have the students stand up and spread out in the room. Direct the students when they have the ball to toss the ball to someone else in the group. As the person catches the ball have them check to see where their pointer finger on their right hand is pointing. Then they need to answer that question or do what it is directing them to do. If more control is needed with the ball toss have the person tossing the ball call the name of the person to whom they are throwing the ball.
- Continue until all have had 1 or 2 times catching and answering questions.

SUGGESTED QUESTIONS BY TOPIC: (Don't forget to add the silly direction.)

- **Getting to know you questions**
  What's your favorite thing about school?
  What do you like to do at home?
  Where is your favorite place you like to go?
  What kind of movies or TV shows do you like to watch?
  Do you have any pets?

- **Anger**
  Show us how to take three deep breaths when you are angry.
  Name one thing you notice happening to your body when you are getting mad.
  Name your top choice of ways to help you calm down when you are mad.
  Share about a time that you got mad.
  Tell us about a time you handled yourself well when you were angry.

- **Friendship**
  Name something nice about you that people like.
  Name a good chit-chat question to use to start talking with others.
  What is good character? How is that important in getting along with others?
  What do you look for in a friend?

- **Study Skills**
  What is your favorite subject and why?
  Where is your best place to study and do your homework?
  How do you handle distractions when you are trying to listen and concentrate?
  What is your advice to someone about how to do well in school?

continued

- **Self Concept**
  Name something that you can do well.
  Tell about something that you have done recently that you feel proud about.
  I feel happy when…
  What do you tell yourself when you make a mistake?

Bouncy Ball

Purpose: An action game that can be used to summarize previously discussed ideas or to gather suggestions or ideas about future topics.

Activity:

- **Materials Needed:** ball to bounce
- Direct the group to stand in a circle with one person with the ball in the middle. The person in the middle needs to bounce the ball to someone in the circle. The person receiving the ball must share something on the specified topic within five seconds and bounce the ball back to the middle. The bouncing and sharing continues until someone is unable to answer within the five second limit, then that person exchanges with the person in the center.

- Possible topics for sharing are:
  things you need to do to be a good listener
  ways to be a good friend
  ways to calm down when you are angry
  ways to get organized

You may choose to add some silly topics to the game such as:
- names that you can name your pet dog
- name the different states in the United States

If You Like...

Purpose: Getting to know you game

Activity: Say: *Listen to the following statements and if it is true about you – follow the directions. Also watch for others and how they answer.*

1. If you have a pet dog, stand on your right foot.
2. If you have a pet cat, stand on your left foot.
3. If you have a different kind of pet, (other than a dog or cat) do a jumping jack.
4. If you like playing football, oink like a pig.
5. If you like singing, touch your ears.
6. If you like to play outside, snap your fingers
7. If you have a brother, raise both hands.
8. If you have a sister, do the twist.
9. If you like pizza, crow like a rooster.
10. If you like ice cream, hoot like an owl.
11. If you like to roller blade, wave hello.
12. If you like to ride bikes, stomp your feet.
13. If you like to play video games, clap your hands over your head.
14. If you're a student at _____ school, smile.

Discuss:
Ask: *What did you see that you had in common with others? What do we all have in common? What are the benefits of getting to know others?*

Toot Your Own Horn

Purpose: An activity to allow students to share something they have done well and are proud of and to experience the accolades of the group.

Activity:
- **Materials Needed:** Kazoos or some type of horn (even a paper birthday horn will work) for each person including the leader
- Take turns going around the circle and have students share either something they are proud of that they do well or have them share something they did well this past week that they are proud of. As each students shares, instruct the others to blow/toot their horn in celebration. Remind students of the importance of recognizing the things they do well as well as supporting others in their successes.

Freeze

Purpose: An active game to practice impulse control.

Activity:

- Instruct students to stand in a circle and begin with yourself as the leader. As the leader you need to make different motions and movements that the group needs to follow such as hands up, down, in, out, feet up, down, bending over, etc. In the middle of the motion the leader needs to stop unexpectedly. When the leader stops everyone else in the group must also stop. The leader then selects another student to lead the group in the motions and then stopping. Allow each member of the group to lead the group.

- Play a second round in which the leader makes different motions the group is to follow but this time the group needs to freeze when the leader says the word "freeze" regardless whether the leader actually stops the action or not.

Discuss:

Ask: *What did you have to do to be successful to "freeze" the motion?* (Elicit such responses as listening, looking, concentrating, willingness for others to be in charge).

Ask: *When would this skill be helpful in everyday life?* (Include: when an adult or someone in authority ask you to stop a behavior).

Balloon Volleyball

Purpose: Active game that involves giving encouraging statements to teammates.

Activity:
- **Materials Needed:** 2 or 3 balloons
- A balloon is tossed in the air and the object is to keep the balloon bouncing in the air. You may have students claim a spot not to move from or have them sit in chairs and play from the seated position. Add two or three balloons at once for the challenge. Play once without talking and then play with students giving each other encouraging, complimentary statements about hitting the balloons.

Discuss:
Ask: *What was the difference between playing without talking and playing with giving encouraging/complimentary statements? How did it feel when someone gave you an encouraging/complimentary statement? How often do we do this for others in real life?*

Go Around Statements

Purpose: To encourage sharing.

Activity: Choose a sentence starter from the list below or create one of your own. Take turns going around the group allowing students to complete the sentence.

SENTENCE STARTERS

ANGER CONTROL:
- I get angry when…
- Today I feel … because…
- Something fun I have done this week is…
- I used to… but now I…
- One thing I have improved on lately is…
- I wish I could…
- When I have something bothering me, I let them know by…
- I am happy when…

FRIENDSHIP:
- I like being with people who…
- I am a good friend because…
- Friends are important because…
- When I'm with friends I like to…
- One way I meet new people is…
- Something I enjoy doing is…

SELF CONCEPT:
- Something I like about myself that I would not change is…
- People who know me well think I am…
- Something I did well last week that I am proud of…
- Something I have done recently to help someone is…
- Something I would like to learn to try is…
- The best thing that happened last week was…

STUDY SKILLS:
- One way I show the teacher that I am listening is…
- I think school is…
- My favorite thing about school is…
- Something I do well in class that I could help others with is…
- I could make better grades if…
- One thing I am getting better at is…
- My teacher thinks that I am…

Questions...Questions

Purpose: Provides a fun way for students to answer questions and share.

Activity:
- **Materials Needed:** Copy and cut apart the Question and Action cards found on the next pages
- **Directions:** Set the Question and Action cards in separate stacks face down. Begin by having a student draw a card from the Question Card stack and answer the question. If they draw a card that says "TAKE AN ACTION CARD" have them draw a card from the Action Card stack and follow the directions on the card. Continue having the students take turns in drawing cards.

Question Card

Question Card

Question Card

Question Card

Question Card

Question Card

Question Card

Question Card

Question Card

Question Card

What is something
that makes you mad?

If you could have
three wishes, what
would they be?

What is something that
makes you sad?

What kind of movies
or TV shows do you like
to watch?

What is something that
makes you angry?

What is a job at
home that you do not
like to do?

What is something that
makes you happy?

What is your favorite
thing to do after
school?

What is something
nice about someone in
the group?

What is your
favorite holiday?

Question Card

Question Card

Question Card

Question Card

Question Card

Question Card

Question Card

Question Card

Question Card

Question Card

TAKE AN ACTION CARD

TAKE AN ACTION CARD

TAKE AN ACTION CARD

TAKE AN ACTION CARD

TAKE AN ACTION CARD

TAKE AN ACTION CARD

What is something about school that you like?

TAKE AN ACTION CARD

What is something you like about yourself?

TAKE AN ACTION CARD

Action Card

Action Card

Action Card

Action Card

Action Card

Action Card

Action Card

Action Card

Action Card

Action Card

Stand on one foot and scratch your head.

Moo like a cow.

Shake hands with everyone in the group.

Snap your fingers twice.

Crow like a rooster.

Make a silly face.

Oink like a pig.

Do three jumping jacks.

Hop like a frog.

Act like a kitten.

Hand Mirroring*

Purpose: Provides a fun approach to practicing the leading and following skills needed in friendships.

Activity:
- Instruct students to pair up facing each other.
- In the pair have the students decide who is to lead first and who is to follow first. You may have them choose the leader by checking to see whose birthday is the closest to the day's date – that person leads first while the other follows.
- Explain that the leader holds their hands out with palms facing their partner. The partner needs to match this position with their palms of their hands facing their partner's – about 3 inches apart. The leader begins moving their hands around while their partner tries to mirror or copy the hand movements with his/her own hands. Instruct the leader to begin with slow, smooth hand movements, then increase the challenge with more animated, creative movements. Once finished, reverse the roles so each pair has a chance to practice leading and following.

Discuss:
Ask the students what skills were needed to follow well? To lead well? Discuss with the students the importance of learning to lead and follow in friendships.

* Adapted with permission from Bowman and Bowman (1998). Individual Counseling. Chapin, South Carolina: YouthLight, Inc.

Anger Management

Anger Management

Feeling angry or mad at times is a natural, normal part of life. However, to be successful in life we need to learn how to manage and deal with our angry feelings in an appropriate way. Anger is an extremely complex feeling with multiple and varied triggers and causes for the individual. Small group counseling activities in this section focus not only on the basic self control skills of anger management but also provide additional skills to reduce the frustration and anger that may be caused by poor interpersonal skills, negative thinking, and lack of skills in handling stress and other problems. The activities also offer a review of how the media and others may influence one's behavior.

Information in this book is provided for you to first assess and determine your group's specific needs and then for you to choose skill building activities from the multiple list that best meets the needs of your group. The first activity in this section Things That Bug Me is a needs assessment activity that collects feedback from the student, teacher, and parent. Once the specific needs of your group are determined then you can use the Correlation Chart on page 58 to select session activities. For each session a main skill building activity needs to be selected as well as an icebreaker/energizer chosen (See Icebreakers/Energizers Section). An additional, optional component can be added to each group session – Service Learning (See the Service Learning Section for more information). The Small Group Roster and Planning Form on pages 19-22 can be helpful in writing down the group plans.

This book is designed in hopes of helping counselors to be focused on students' needs and to be efficient and effective in helping students.

Anger Management Group Activities

• INITIAL GROUP SESSION...

Review the Getting Started: First Group Session on page 17. Complete the Needs Assessment Activity A which includes a student and a parent/teacher needs assessment. Review the areas of need from these assessments and with the use of the Needs Assessment Correlation to Skill Building Activities Chart on page 58, plan the skill building activities for the remaining group sessions.

• SKILL BUILDING ACTIVITIES...

The following is a list of Anger Management Skill building activities grouped by sub topics that relate to the needs assessment. Each activity will take about 20-25 minutes therefore only one activity needs to be planned for each group meeting. Not all activities will be used, only those which relate to the needs of your group. Select your activities, guided by your Needs Assessment Correlation to Skill Building Activities Chart on page 58. You may also want to use the Small Group Roster and Planning Chart on pages 19-22 to organize your sessions and activities.

Bothered by Other Problems

Influences

• CLOSING GROUP SESSION...

Review the How to End: Final Group Session on page 23. Complete the Closing Group Activity A10 which includes a student and a parent/teacher post assessment. Use this information to evaluate the group and to determine follow up with individual students on continuing weaknesses.

NEEDS ASSESSMENT ACTIVITY A
Things That Bug Me

PURPOSE: To provide a creative format to assess the needs of the students in the group as it relates to anger.

MATERIALS NEEDED:
- Eight plastic bugs with the information on Things That Bug Me Activity Sheet taped to the bugs OR the bugs on the sheet cut out. Place the plastic or paper bugs in a jar.
- Student Needs Assessment sheet copied for each student.

PROCEDURE:

1. **Introduction:** Ask: *How many of you have ever been on a picnic, camping trip, or just playing outside and the mosquitoes or other bugs start flying around you and bothering you?* Elaborate on how bugs can become a problem. In the discussion, relate these bugs to things in life that may happen that bother us and make us mad. Give an example the students can relate to. Ask the students to give other examples of things that may "bug" people or make people angry. Encourage sharing.

2. Hand each student a Needs Assessment Sheet and place the bug jar in the center of the group area. Tell the students that these bugs have a message about different things that may happen in life that may bug people. Have the students take turns pulling a bug from the jar and reading it to the group. The group leader may assist in the reading of the information if necessary. The leader needs to facilitate a discussion/explanation of the statement on each bug asking such questions as:

   What do you think that means? What would a person be thinking, doing, or saying if that "bugged" them?

   Have you ever seen anyone who you think was being "bugged" by that? Don't give any names, but what did you see or hear that made you think that was bugging them?

   How about you – is this something that has "bugged" you before?

3. As the bugs are pulled from the jar and discussed, direct the students to find the number on their Needs Assessment sheet (refer to the number on the bug) and circle to what extent this bugs them.

4. **Closure:** Encourage the students to tune in to the things that bug them during the week. Sharing that awareness is the first step to dealing with these bugs.

   Explain to the students that you have a similar assessment for their parent and/or teacher to complete. Send copies with the students to give to their Parent/Teacher to complete and return. Or you may choose to put the Needs Assessment in teachers' boxes and mail to parents.

Things That Bug Me Activity Sheet

Directions: Cut out the bugs (or get plastic bugs and tape the information on them) and place in a jar. Have students pull a bug from the jar and read about the different things you get mad at or that "bug" you. Discuss and allow students to complete the number on the Needs Assessment sheet that correlates with the number on the bug.

2 I get "bugged" when there are conflicts and disagreements with my friends.

4 I get "bugged" when I am left out.

1 When things bug me and I get mad, I just react without thinking and I usually say or do the wrong thing that gets me in more trouble.

3 I get "bugged" when people tease me.

5 I get "bugged" when I feel like I can't do anything right.

7 I get "bugged" when I feel things are unfair.

6 I get "bugged" when my parents or teachers correct my behavior.

8 I get "bugged" more when I am worried about other problems.

9 I get "bugged" by all of the violence on TV and video games.

10 I get "bugged" by how other people I know handle their anger.

STUDENT NEEDS ASSESSMENT
for Managing Anger

Name: _____

	STRONGLY AGREE	AGREE	DISAGREE	STRONGLY DISAGREE
1. When angry I am able to use self-control. I am able to stay in control with what I say and do even though I am angry.	4	3	2	1
2. I handle disagreements with my friends well.	4	3	2	1
3. I handle being teased or picked on by others well.	4	3	2	1
4. I can handle being left out well.	4	3	2	1
5. I like how I think, feel, and act.	4	3	2	1
6. When parents or teachers correct my behavior, I handle it well.	4	3	2	1
7. When I feel things are unfair, I handle it well.	4	3	2	1
8. When I am worried about other problems I find good ways to deal with them so I can handle situations well and not have my anger get out of control.	4	3	2	1
9. I monitor what I watch on TV and the video games I play so that I am not exposed to too much violence.	4	3	2	1
10. The people in my life handle their anger well.	4	3	2	1

PARENT/TEACHER NOTE
Needs Assessment

Dear Teacher/Parent,

Feeling angry or mad at times is a natural, normal part of life. However, in order to be successful in life we need to learn how to manage and deal with our angry feelings in an appropriate way. In our small group on Anger Management we will explore the triggers of our anger and then build the skills to handle that area more effectively. In order to structure our small group to meet the specific needs of the group members, I need your input. Please take some time to review the child's behavior over the past month, complete the needs assessment given below and return. Please feel free to add comments or to share any information that would be helpful as we begin our small group. Thank you for your input as we work together to help our students be their best.

Sincerely,

Your Child's Counselor

PARENT/TEACHER NEEDS ASSESSMENT FOR

STUDENT/CHILD'S NAME _____

	STRONGLY AGREE	AGREE	DISAGREE	STRONGLY DISAGREE
1. When angry he/she is able to use self-control – able to stay in control with what he/she says and does even though he/she is angry.	4	3	2	1
2. He/she handles disagreements with his/her friends well.	4	3	2	1
3. He/she handles being teased or picked on by others well.	4	3	2	1
4. He/she can handle being left out well.	4	3	2	1
5. He/she likes how he/she thinks, feels, and acts.	4	3	2	1
6. When parents or teachers correct his/her behavior he/she handles it well.	4	3	2	1
7. When he/she feels things are unfair he/she handles it well.	4	3	2	1
8. When he/she is worried about other problems he/she can still handle his/her anger well.	4	3	2	1
9. He/she monitors what they watch and play on TV and video games so as not to be exposed to too much violence.	4	3	2	1
10. The people in his/her life handle their anger well.	4	3	2	1

Comments:

NEEDS ASSESSMENT CORRELATION
to Anger Management Skill Building Activities

Directions: Use the chart to assist in planning skill building activities for group sessions. Below is a listing of the activities as they relate to each statement in the needs assessment. Select an appropriate skill building activity for each session depending on the needs determined from the assessments as well as group discussions and observations. Area of needs may be indicated by a score of '1' or '2' on an item on the assessment. For area of heavy need you may choose to plan for several sessions utilizing several skill building activities focusing on that sub topic. For lighter needs you may choose only one session selecting only one skill building activity from that sub topic. If there is no need indicated for that sub topic then do not plan to use a skill building activity from that area. Remember these skill building activities are written covering a wide range of information but are intended for you to choose only the ones that fit the group's needs. All activities will not be used in a typical 6-8 session group. Note that most skill building activities for Anger Management are marked by the letter A indicating this section of the book, however at times a skill building activity in another section will be referenced and will be indicated by a different section letter.

NEEDS ASSESSMENT STATEMENTS

SKILL BUILDING ACTIVITIES THAT CORRELATE

Needs Assessment Statement							
1. When angry I am able to use self-control. lable to stay in control with what I say and do even though I am angry.	A1.1	A1.2	A1.3	A1.4	A1.5	C1.2	C1.3
2. I can handle disagreements with his/her friends well.	A2.1	A2.2	A2.3	B4.3	B5.3		
3. I can handle being teased or picked on by others well.	A3.1	A3.2	D2.3				
4. I can handle being left out well.	A4.1	B5.1					
5. I like how I think, feel, and act.	A5.1	A5.2	D1.1	D1.2	D1.3	D3.2	D3.3
6. When parents or teachers correct my behavior, I handle it well.	A6.1						
7. When I feel things are unfair I handle it well.	A7.1						
8. When I am worried about other problems I can still handle my anger well.	A8.1	A8.2	D2.1	D2.2	D2.4	D2.5	
9. I monitor what I watch on TV and video games I play so as not to be exposed to too much violence.	A9.1						
10. The people in my life handle their anger well.	A0.2						

58

ACTIVITY A1.1
In Control

PURPOSE: To be aware of what happens to your body when you are angry and to learn ways to calm yourself down.

MATERIALS NEEDED:
• Body Cues activity cards cut apart
• Calming Down Activity sheet – one for each student

PROCEDURE:
1. **Introduction:** Ask each student to think for a moment about what happens to their body when they get really angry. Allow for sharing.

2. Turn the pictures of the Body Cues face down and have each student pick a card. Ask them to review the card and to explain to the group how their picture shows what happens to your body when you are angry. Facilitate a discussion asking such questions as: Have you ever noticed your body doing that when you are angry? Does it make your problem worse or better if you allow your body to continue reacting to your anger - explain? Have you been able to catch your anger in time and calm down when you feel your body getting out of control? What have you found helps you calm down when you feel angry?

3. Give each student a Calming Down Activity sheet. Tell the students that when our body starts to react to being mad we need to calm down and get in control so that we do not make things worse. Have the students complete the activity sheet and share. Allow and encoourage students to add additional information to their sheet that is learned through group discussion.

4. Place the Body Cue cards face down and take turns having the students draw a card and act out the picture. Have the students guess which body reaction to anger the person is role playing and then have the student share a strategy for calming the body down.

5. **Closure:** Encourage the students during the week to tune into their body cues to help them calm down so that they can respond appropriately in a controlled way rather than to react in an out of control way. Ask them to take their Calming Down activity sheet home and share with their parent. To encourage this you may choose to say that if they return their sheet signed by a parent then they may choose a surprise from your treasure box! (Of course this means you may have to create a treasure box but the pay off is the student having the incentive to continue thinking about what they learned in group. To then have them tell and show their parent may be worth it.)

Body Cues Activity Cards

Directions: Cut the cards apart. Draw a card and explain how the picture on the card is reacting to angry feelings.

Closed due to technical difficulties — Thinking Shuts Down	Clenched Jaw
Fast Breathing	Pounding Heart
Tight Fists	Face on Fire
Butterflies in Stomach	Knot in Chest

Calming Down Activity Sheet

Directions: Complete the following with information on ways to help our body calm down when we are mad.

Tell yourself to:

_____

_____

_____

Slow your breathing down by:

_____

_____

_____

Do something okay with your hands like:

_____

_____

_____

Do something active like:

_____

_____

_____

Other things I can do to calm down:

_____

_____

_____

_____

_____

ACTIVITY A1.2
Rules for Handling Anger

PURPOSE: To establish basic guidelines for managing our anger.

MATERIALS NEEDED:
- Chart paper and marker
- (Optional): *Lightening Gel* that can be purchased from YouthLight (1-800-209-9774); a plastic cup; pointed scissors, water, and a bowl

PROCEDURE:
1. **Introduction:** Ask the students to think of all types of things they know that have rules (board games, classroom, driving a car, sports games, etc.). Choose a specific example they have shared and discuss by asking: *What if there were no rules in …?* Join in the fun thinking about the freedom of no rules but then bring up the problems that could arise if there were no rules. Talk about the responsibility of considering others and summarize that rules are important to help things work smoothly and for all to work, play, and live well together.

2. Ask the group to think about when people get angry. Ask: *Does the anger ever hurt anyone? Can it keep us from getting along well with others? What can happen if the anger is out of control?* Ask the group to help you create rules for handling anger. (The following three rules may be a guideline: 1. Do not hurt yourself. 2. Do not hurt others. 3. Do not hurt property.) As you create these anger management rules or similar rules, write them on chart paper to be displayed and referred back to during your group discussions. (For more information on rules of anger management refer to the "Madness Management" section in *Coping with Conflict: An "Elementary" Approach* by Senn and Sitsch, Youthlight, Inc. 1-800- 209-9774).

3. To practice following the rules defined above, create "What if" situations such as:
   - If someone is mad at someone and he/she calls that person a name, what would happen? Does it follow the rules?
   - If someone is mad about something but he/she holds it in and does nothing and says nothing about it, what would happen? Does it follow the rules?
   - If someone is mad at his/her parents and he/she messes up his/her room and breaks things, what would happen? Does it follow the rules?
   - If someone is mad at someone and he/she tries to get back at that person by spreading rumors, what would happen? Does it follow the rules?

4. (Optional) Using the *Lightening Gel*, plastic cup, water, scissors, and bowl, do the following to demonstrate what happens when anger gets out of control:
   - Hold the plastic cup up and ask the students to share things that happen that can make you mad. As the students share, poke holes in the plastic cup with the point of the scissors.
   - Pretend to pour water in the cup with holes and talk about how it would make a total mess of things. Remind students that the holes in the cup stand for their anger and that as they go about their day if they don't do anything about their anger, don't follow the anger management rules

and let it get out of control, then it will make a mess of things. Demonstrate pouring the water in the cup but put the bowl under the cup to catch the water so it doesn't make as much of a mess.

- Propose to the students that following the rules is needed along with finding good ways to deal with that anger so that we don't make a mess of things. Hold up the *Lightening Gel* and explain that this stands for the "stuff" in us that helps us follow the anger management rules and deal with our anger appropriately. Repeat pouring the water in the cup with holes but quickly add the *Lightening Gel.* The powder will solidify the water, no longer making a mess. Relate this to when we follow the rules and find good ways to deal with our anger we keep from making a mess of our lives. (Caution: Do not allow the students to touch the the gel: It is harmful to eyes or if ingested.) Lead into a discussion reviewing the rules and discussing strategies to managing our anger.

5. **Closure:** Have students memorize and/or write on paper to take with them the anger management rules the group has created. Challenge them to double check to see if they are following the rules of anger management when a situation arises.

Get the group's agreement for you to send out a brief note to teachers and/or parents sharing their group rules of anger management that they have created. The purpose of the note is to engage the adult's help to encourage and support the child in the new information they are learning and to reinforce these skills as they see their child using them.

Dear Parent/Teacher:

In group this week we created guidelines or rules to follow in order to handle our anger well. Our rules of anger management are:

_____

_____

_____

_____

We need your help to encourage and support your child in following their rules when they are angry. If he/she is breaking a rule when they are angry such as, (add an appropriate example that relates to your group's rules), then ask him/her if what he/she just did or said broke one of the rules and ask the child what he/she could do differently. When your child does handle anger within the rules listed, reinforce this with a compliment pointing out what he/she did well.

Thank you for your continued support as we work together.

Sincerely,

Your Child's Counselor

ACTIVITY A1.3
Positive Thinking

PURPOSE: To develop an awareness that people can choose how to look at or think about a situation and that choosing to think in a positive way about a situation will help decrease angry feelings.

MATERIALS NEEDED:
- Perception picture
- Positive Thinking Activity sheet with pictures enlarged and laminated
- Erasable Dry Erase marker for yourself and each student
- Parent/Teacher note for each student

PROCEDURE:

1. **Introduction:** Show the perception picture of the Beautiful Lady/Witch. If students are having difficulty seeing only one, talk them through it giving them pointers and hints to seeing the other part of the picture. Process what it took in order to see the different picture: a willingness to see the other side? an open mind? patience? willingness to listen to others? effort? Share that our mind is very powerful and we can use it in good ways to help us with our feelings. When we are mad, we can look at or think about the situation in a different way that can help us feel better about the problem. Our thoughts affect our feelings, and the good news is that we are in charge of our thoughts.

2. From the Positive Thinking Activity sheet select one positive thinking card and one negative thinking card (may choose to use the thumbs up and thumbs down rather than positive and negative). Hold up the positive card and discuss why it is a positive way to think about the situation and how you would feel. Using a dry erase marker, on the back of the positive statement card draw a smiley face. Next hold up the negative thinking card and discuss how that would make you feel if you continued to think about it in that way. Then turn the back of the card over and with the help of the group rewrite the negative thinking to a positive thinking statement.

3. Hand out the remaining cards to the students and have them review their card – help with the reading if needed. Instruct the students to decide whether it is positive or negative thinking. Have them turn to the back of the card and draw a smiley face for positive thinking or to rewrite the negative statement to a positive statement. Have students share their cards and discuss.

4. Pull out a blank situation/thinking card and have the students think back through their week for a situation they may have been involved in - either positive or negative – and write down their situation and their thinking. (If their thinking was negative have the group help in rewriting it to a positive statement before adding it to the card). Summarize that positive thinking helps maintain positive feelings which helps minimize angry feelings. You may choose to display these for the group and use them in the review for your next visit.

continued

5. **Closure:** Challenge the students to be more aware of their thoughts about situations that arise so that you can choose positive thoughts. Ask the students to take home a letter to their parent/teacher sharing the information that you learned today. Part of the letter has several blank cut apart situation/thinking slips. Ask the students to complete these with situations that come up for them during the week. If they handled a situation with positive thinking have them write that on the sheet. If they used negative thinking have them write it down but then on the back have them rewrite it to a positive statement. Provide incentives for bringing these back completed.

PARENT/TEACHER NOTE
Positive Thinking

Dear Parent/Teacher,

Today in group we talked about how we choose to look at and think about a situation and how it impacts the way we feel about a problem. Negative thoughts about problems often increase our angry feelings about the situation. Therefore, we worked on rewriting our thoughts to positive thoughts. If your child is in the habit of thinking about the negative in situations then it will take lots of practice, support, and encouragement to change to positive thinking. But with the child's hard work and the support from home and school your child can be successful.

At the bottom of this note are cut apart Situation/Thinking Cards that the students are asked to complete with situations that arise during their week. If they handle the situation with positive thinking have them write that on the sheet. If they used negative thinking have them write it down but then on the back help them rewrite it to a positive statement. Take time with your child each day to evaluate how they chose to think about different situations. Make sure to compliment with specifics when they use positive thinking or even when they are able to go back later and tell how they could have thought about it in a positive way. Compliment them on using their good thinking power to help them feel better about difficult situations.

Thank you for your support as we work together.

Sincerely,

Your Child's Counselor

SITUATION:

_____

_____

_____

_____

SITUATION:

_____

_____

_____

_____

Perception Picture

Positive Thinking Activity Sheet

Preparation: Enlarge, cut apart and laminate the following situation/thinking bubbles.

Directions: Students are to read the situations and thought bubbles to decide whether they are examples of positive thinking or negative thinking. If one is positive thinking, students are to draw a smiley face on the back with an erasable marker. If one is negative thinking, students need to rewrite the negative thinking to positive thinking on the back of the card.

SITUATION:
My best friend went off with someone else at recess to play and left me out.

I'll show her. I'll start a bad rumor about her and tell everyone how mean she is.

SITUATION:
In class we had to partner up with someone else and my best friend didn't choose me as a partner.

That's okay. This will give me a chance to get to know someone else a little better.

SITUATION:
Even though I raised my hand the teacher didn't call on me.

The teacher doesn't like me – she/he never has.

Positive Thinking Activity Sheet

SITUATION:
I didn't get elected to serve on student council.

Nobody likes me – something must be wrong with me.

SITUATION:
The teacher put my name on the board for talking.

I need to listen to the warning, quit talking and focus back on my work.

SITUATION:
I got a 50 on my math paper.

I'll never be able to learn this!

SITUATION:
Tonya said that Mary said that Lucy said that my outfit was ugly.

I'm so embarassed – I'll never wear this outfit again.

70

Positive Thinking Activity Sheet

SITUATION:
Mom said I had time out because I was fussing with my brother.

It's true I was fussing with my brother. It may help to sit awhile, calm down, and figure out a better way.

SITUATION:
Mom won't take my friend and me to the skating rink this afternoon

That's okay, we'll play video games instead and maybe she can take us next week.

SITUATION:

_____
_____
_____
_____

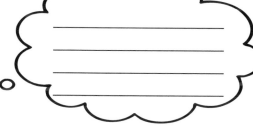

SITUATION:

_____
_____
_____
_____

ACTIVITY A1.4
Squeeze Balloon

PURPOSE: To make and take a squeeze balloon and to learn how to use the squeeze balloon to reduce angry feelings.

MATERIALS NEEDED:
- Need helium quality balloons for each group member
- For each group member you need an empty single size soft drink bottle filled with flour or baking soda (this is used for the filler in the balloons). Prepare these bottles before the group meeting – a funnel may help add the ingredient.
- Permanent fine line markers for writing on the balloons
- Chart paper and marker

PROCEDURE:
1. **Introduction:** Ask the students if they ever squished a ball or clay (playdoh) in their hands when they were angry to help get angry feelings out. Explain to the students that it can help but that it is not only squeezing the ball but also what you say in your head while you are squeezing the ball that can help reduce angry feelings. Think together and make a list on chart paper of things that would help to say or think in your head to get rid of angry feelings and calm down. Include such things as: calm down, chill…, think happy, take a deep breath, etc.

2. Share with the students that today in group they are going to make a squeeze ball to use to help them calm down when they are angry. Give each student a balloon and the bottle of baking soda/flour. Instruct them to carefully put the mouth of the balloon over the mouth of the bottle. Next turn the bottle upside down so that the baking soda/flour begins to go into the balloon. Work carefully with your hands - shaking the bottle and stretching and packing the baking soda/flour into the balloon. When the balloon is large enough to squeeze in your fist, remove the balloon from the bottle and tie a knot in the top. Help all students complete this. Caution them that the balloon is only for squeezing and that it can break if it is treated too roughly.

3. Have the students select one or several of the calming down words that you listed in step 1. Have the students write those words they select on the outside of the squeeze ball with a permanent marker.

4. Role play by sharing an angry situation and have the students pretend to begin to get angry. Then have the students pick up their squeeze ball to begin squeezing it and repeating their calming words while they are calming down.

5. **Closure:** Allow them to take their squeeze balloons with them with the understanding that they will need to keep it in their desk or book bag unless they get permission from their teacher. You may choose to discuss with teacher ahead of time – some teachers will prefer that this be put away while others will encourage their use in the classroom. Challenge the students to use the squeeze balloon and the calming words in real life when they feel themselves beginning to get angry.

ACTIVITY A1.5
The Chill Cube

PURPOSE: To brainstorm strategies for managing anger.

MATERIALS NEEDED:
• Chart paper and a marker
• Chill Cube activity sheet for each student
• Scissors, tape, pencils, crayons, colored markers

PROCEDURE:

1. **Introduction:** Ask students to think about a time that they have been really mad and yet were able to calm down and get their anger under control. Ask: *What did you find that helped you calm down?*

2. On chart paper write down the suggestions of good ways to calm down when you are angry. Include the following:
   • Take several deep breaths
   • Talk to an adult or friend you trust
   • Do something active like jump rope, play basketball, jog, do jumping jacks
   • Tell yourself to calm down
   • Write the problem down and think it through
   • Imagine a peaceful place
   • Listen to music
   • Count to 10
   • Walk away from the problem
   • Remind yourself of the consequences for anger out of control
   • Distract yourself by doing something fun
   • Talk it out with the person in a calm way

3. Hand out The Chill Cube Activity Sheet to each student. Have the students choose their top six strategies of managing anger from the list that was brainstormed by the group. In the three squares across the top and the center squares going down the middle ask the students to write and illustrate their top six strategies. Provide pencils, crayons and markers.

4. As they finish their cube with the writing and illustrations, have them follow the directions to cut the cube out along the dotted lines and fold on the solid lines until it forms the shape of a cube. Tape the sides together for reinforcement.

5. Allow the students to take turns rolling their cube and explaining/demonstrating for the group how that strategy can be helpful in managing anger.

6. **Closure:** Ask the students to take home a note to their parent/teacher sharing the information that they learned today. Ask the student to also show and tell their parent/teacher about their Chill Cube. You may choose to give an incentive if the student's get their note signed by a parent or teacher. Encourage the students to use their cube to focus on good ways to calm down.

The Chill Cube Activity Sheet

Directions: In the three squares across the top and the center squares going down write and illustrate your top six strategies to calming down when you are angry. Then cut out along the dotted lines and fold along the solid lines. Fold in the shape of a cube and tape together. When you begin to feel angry turn to the chill cube to roll an idea to help you calm down.

PARENT/TEACHER NOTE
The Chill Cube

Dear Parent/Teacher,

In group today we talked about different strategies for calming down when we are angry. To help remind us of those strategies we made a Chill Cube. Ask your child to share his/her cube with you explaining or demonstrating how each strategy works.

Encourage your child to use those strategies indicated on the Chill Cube. When there is a problem and your child is starting to get angry refer him/her to the Chill Cube in order to pick a strategy to help calm down. Compliment your child when he/she is using good strategies.

Being a good role model is always a good way to teach your child. At times when you start to get mad, ask your child if you can borrow the Chill Cube to pick a strategy to use. And then talk out loud about your choice and how you are using it to calm down.

Thank you for your support as we work together.

Sincerely,

Your Child's Counselor

ACTIVITY A2.1
Unlocking Friendship Problems

PURPOSE: To gain skills/strategies in managing friendship problems.

MATERIALS NEEDED:
- Chart paper and markers
- Copy and cut apart cards on the Unlocking Friendship Matching Game and then copy additional game sheets for each student
- Scissors and small plastic bags for each student.

PROCEDURE:

1. **Introduction:** Share with the students that problems in getting along with others are a normal part of life and you have a choice – to get mad about it or to turn your brain on and come up with solutions to those problems. Explain that today we will look at finding the keys to unlock the friendship problems.

2. As a group make a list on chart paper of typical friendship problems that occur. On a second list brainstorm different strategies that can be used to solve and/or manage the problems. Include in your list: share, take turns, postpone, get help, apologize, luck or chance to decide, work it out, and send an "I" message. Draw a large key at the top of this list. Share that the key stands for finding a good way to unlock a problem – a way to handle the problem.

3. Using the cut apart cards from the game sheet, play the Unlocking Friendship Matching Game. Follow the directions given. While you play, make use of the opportunity to share and discuss.

4. **Closure:** Offer the students a copy of the matching game to take home to play with family members or friends. Hand out sheets and allow them to cut apart their cards and place in a small plastic bag to take home. You may choose to add the parent/teacher note to the bag that includes an area to sign and return indicating that they have played the game at home. Offer an incentive for practicing the game at home and returning the note signed. As always, challenge the students to use these strategies in real life situations.

Unlocking Friendship Matching Game

Game Directions: Copy the sheet front/back, cut apart, and set out the cards on a table area face down. Each player takes a turn to turn over 2 cards trying to match the example with the strategy. For example, "Let's get an adult to help us deal with this," is an example of GET HELP. If the two cards the player turned over match, then they get to take the pair and have another turn. If the pair does not match then they need to be turned back over for the next player to try. There are four inappropriate examples of how to handle problems. These four will have no matches and if a player turns one of these over he loses that turn. The player with the most matches technically wins but everyone wins if good problem solving skills are reinforced.

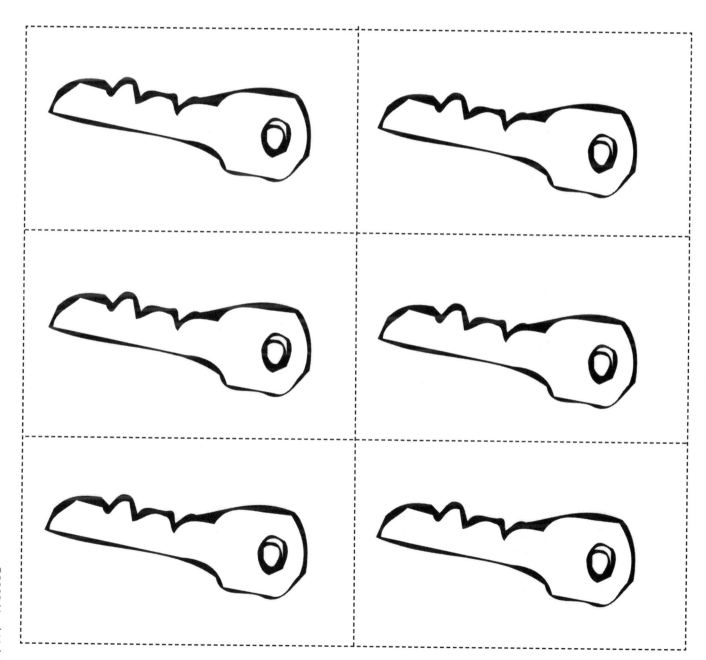

Unlocking Friendship Matching Game

C

"Let's share."

F

"Let's take turns."

B

"Let's get an adult to help us deal with this."

E

"I'm sorry we are having a problem getting along."

A

"Let's flip a coin or draw straws to see who goes first."

D

"Can we work this out?"

Unlocking Friendship Matching Game

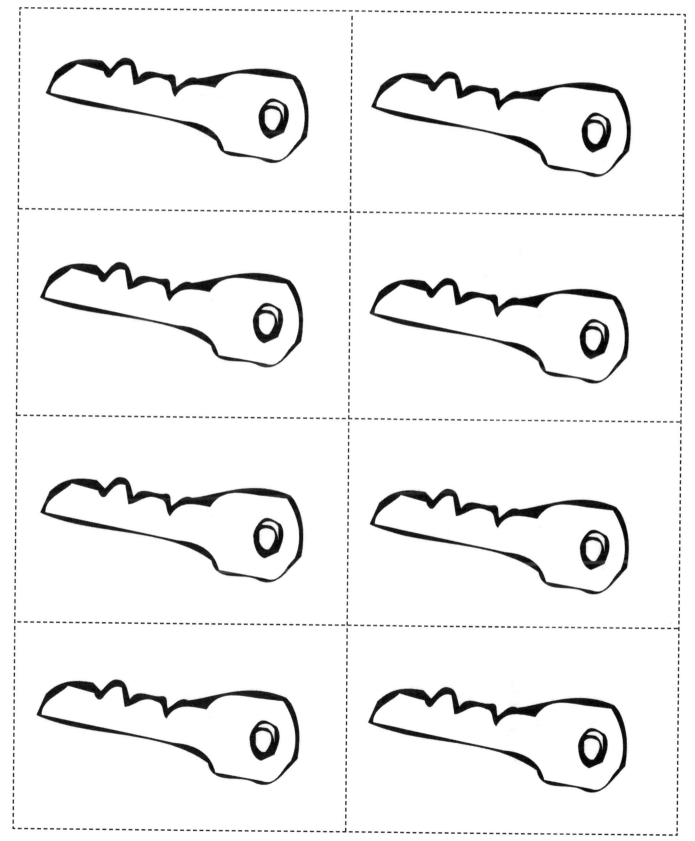

Unlocking Friendship Matching Game

I

"I'm willing to give in some if you are?"

H

"Let's wait and deal with this tomorrow when we are not so upset."

G

"I feel bothered when you have your stuff on my desk. Please keep it over on your own desk."

"That's mine give it to me!"

"I want to go first!"

"We are going to do it my way!"

"It's all your fault!"

C

Share

Unlocking Friendship Matching Game

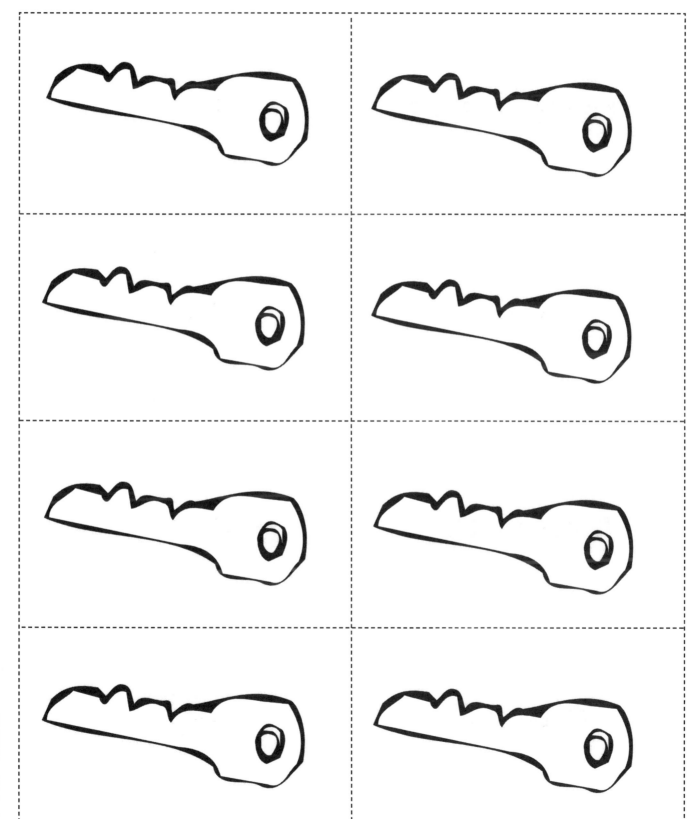

Unlocking Friendship Matching Game

TAKE TURNS

F

'I' MESSAGE

G

GET HELP

B

POSTPONE

H

APOLOGIZE

E

COMPROMISE

I

CHANCE

A

WORK IT OUT

D

PARENT/TEACHER NOTE
Unlocking Friendship Problems

Dear Parent/Teacher,

Today in group we discussed how it is normal to have problems arise in getting along with others but that we have a choice to either get mad and make the problem worse or to find a good way to deal with the problem. We talked about the following strategies:

SHARE – Find a way to use and enjoy together.

TAKE TURNS – Allow each to have a turn so both/all can enjoy.

CHANCE – Flip a coin, draw straws, or any other such luck device to help decide.

POSTPONE – Delay or put off dealing with the problem if one or both are too angry or too tired to deal with it well.

APOLOGIZE – Say "I'm sorry" if you did something wrong or can say, "I'm sorry we're having this problem" in order to help defuse the situation.

WORK IT OUT – Calmly discuss the problem sharing feelings and ideas.

GET HELP – If a problem is escalating, it is sometimes necessary to seek the help of a trusted adult.

"I" MESSAGE – To share in an appropriate way how you are feeling and what you want. It has three steps:
I feel_____ when you_____. Please _____.

COMPROMISE – Both sides can give in some of what they want in order to meet the other in the middle.

We reviewed these strategies in our "Unlocking Friendship Matching Game". A copy of this game is being sent home for you to play together. Game directions are given on the sheet. Find time to play this game with your child – include family and/or friends. Point out and compliment your child when he/she is using these strategies in real life to handle problems. Thanks for your continued support as we work together.

Sincerely,

Your Child's Counselor

Mark below to indicate that your child has participated in playing the game this week.

(Child's name)_____ played the game this week _____ times.

_____
Parent's Signature

Comments:

ACTIVITY A2.2
Tell It With Words!

PURPOSE: To empower students to use words to express themselves and to handle their problems in a positive way (sending "I" messages.)

MATERIALS NEEDED:
- WHAT?WHY?HOW? 'I' message activity sheets copied and put together for each group member. Follow the directions given on the sheet.
- 1x 6 inch slips of paper for each student
- "I" message activity sheet
- Pair of dice
- Tape

PROCEDURE:

1. **Introduction:** Propose the question to the students as to which way will get them what they want the best and with the least amount of complications – using words or using their fists and feet? As the group explores this, present various questions such as: If you think fists and feet - what are the complications? The backlash? If feet and fist are used, do you think there is that feeling of power and triumph – does it come at a cost? How do you think the victim feels? What do you think it would do to the relationship/friendship? Are using words easy? How do using words affect the relationship/friendship? Tell the students that today the group will look at how to use words to handle problems. Share with them that they will be practicing sending "I" messages.

2. Distribute an assembled What?Why?How? "I" message sheet to each student.

3. Ask the students to lift the first question flap – WHAT? Read the information on the inside. Emphasize that figuring out how you feel and being able to tell others is an important step to working out the problem. Brainstorm different feeling words and have them write the words on the outer edge of their letter "I".

4. Continue with opening and reading the WHY? flap and then the HOW? flap and discuss. Present several hypothetical problems to work through the steps of the "I" message together.

5. Next have the students write down a problem from last week or create a typical problem in which an "I" message would be helpful. Have them write their problem on 1x 6 inch piece of paper. As they finish, quickly proof to make sure the problem is acceptable to discuss in group and then tape each one inside a box on the "I" message activity sheet in numbers 8-12. (See page 88).

6. Students now get a chance to practice sending "I" messages using this "I" message activity sheet. Have each group member take a turn rolling the pair of dice. The number rolled on the dice is the number of their pretend problem that they need to create an "I" message and share with the group.

7. **Closure:** Encourage the students to take their "I" message with them and to use "I" messages in real life to see the power they have.

WHAT? WHY? HOW?
'I' Message Activity Sheet

Directions to assemble the 'I' message sheet:

1. Copy page 86 and page 87 preferably on cardstock. Copy on the front side only.

2. Cut out along the solid lines on page 86 and page 87 (leave the dotted lines to fold back the flap during the activity).

3. Place the first page 'I' on top of the second page 'I'. Staple, paste, or tape together the outer edges only.

WHAT?

WHY?

HOW?

An 'I' message is a way of telling others how you feel and what you want in a direct, non-blaming way.

It provides a way to tell people how you feel without being rude, gives you a way to ask for what you want or need, provides a way to talk out conflicts with others, and a way to speak up for yourself in an acceptable way.

Name _____

I feel _____

When you _____

Please _____

'I' Message Activity Sheet

Directions: Add the students' own problem situations that they wrote in Procedure Step 5 to boxes 8-12. Practice sending 'I' messages for the following problems. Roll the dice and check the number below that corresponds with the number on the dice. Create an 'I' message for that problem and role play for the group.

1. Mark took your pencil without asking.

3 You are in class trying to do your seatwork and Jamar keeps making noises with his pencil.

4. You are lining up for lunch and Cindy cuts in front of you.

5. Alex sits next to you and always has his books on your desk.

6. Your little brother Gary always gets into your room and messes it up.

7. Lyn who sits next to you in class keeps bugging you when you're trying to do your work.

ADD YOUR OWN!

8.

9.

10.

11.

12.

ACTIVITY A2.3

Work It Out... *

PURPOSE: To provide a guideline for students to use in order to work through problems with friends.

MATERIALS NEEDED:
• Work It Out Activity Sheet copied on red paper and hearts cut out for each student.

PROCEDURE:

1. **Introduction:** Ask: *Have you ever been mad at a friend and later discovered that it was all a misunderstanding and the friend didn't really do what you thought? Or later you find out why the friend wanted that or said that and you understood better?* Share with the group that problems do come up between people, even the best of friends, because each person is different with different thoughts, feelings and needs. We need to learn to take time to talk things through – talking and listening – so that we can work things out.

2. First share with the group that they are going to learn about how to be a good listener. Set the scene by asking the group to watch you to see if you are being a good listener. For each of the examples below you need to role play inappropriate listening first, discuss with the students, and then role play appropriate listening. Ask for volunteers to role play talking with you. You may choose to assign one of the following topics to talk about - their favorite movie, where they like to go, what they like to do at home in the afternoons, tell about a pet if they have one.

   a. First listening exercise: as they begin talking send the message with your body language that you're not listening – yawn, turn your body away, fidget, etc. Discuss if it was good listening and have them tell the better way. Role play again emphasizing body turned toward, sitting still, and good eye contact.

   b. Second listening exercise: as they begin talking interrupt with your own story. Discuss. Then role play again however sitting quietly but using head nods and uh-huh's. When they have finished sharing their story say something back that showed you listened – either summarize or ask an open question.

   Have the students pair up and take turns talking and listening. Give them a prompt to talk about. Have them use the good listening skills of sitting quietly, good eye contact, head nods, uh-huh's, and saying something back that shows you listened. Emphasize that when there are problems in getting along it is important to be a good listener in talking out the problem – there are two sides to every story.

3. Explain that the second part of working a problem through is knowing how to talk and tell your thoughts and feelings about the situation in a non blaming way. "I" messages are good for this. If you have not taught "I" messages then spend some extra time going over this on the Work It Out Activity sheet.

continued

4. Give each person a cut out heart from the Work it Out Activity sheet. Review the rules and guidelines for working out a problem. Emphasize how listening, talking in a non-blaming way, and being creative to work out the problem are important.

5. Brainstorm together typical problems in getting along and have students pair up and practice the Working it Out using the rules and guidelines given.

6. **Closure:** Encourage students to use these guidelines and try them in real life.

Adapted with permission from Senn and Sitsch (1996) Coping with Conflict An "Elementary" Approach. Chapin, SC: YouthLight, Inc.

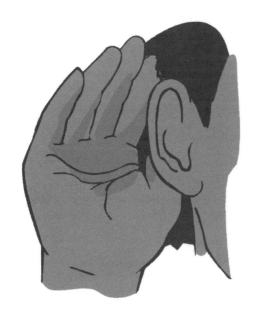

WORK IT OUT

(the heart is to remind you to talk and listen in a caring way)

RULES:
1. Both people must want to work out or solve the problem.
2. Do not interrupt. Take turns talking and listening.
3. No name-calling or blaming.
4. Be as honest as you can without hurting feelings.

GUIDELINES:

Each person takes turns talking and listening.

1. The talker first sends an "I" message:

Name_____

I feel _____ when you _____.

Please _____.

The listener listens well using:
Eye contact
Head nods
A summary (saying something back that shows you are listening)

Change roles so that each person has a chance to talk and listen.

2. Next, each person gives suggestions to solve the problem.

Ex. "Maybe we should try _____

_____."

3. Then, choose from the suggestions to solve
the problem.

ACTIVITY A3.1
Teasing...Why?

PURPOSE: To provide an understanding and awareness of the reasons people tease others.

MATERIALS NEEDED:
• Chart paper and markers

PROCEDURE:

1. **Introduction:** Define teasing as to annoy, say or do mean things, or make fun of someone in a joking way. Ask how a person might feel when they are being teased. Answers can range anywhere from happy (remember some teasing can be friendly where both people are having fun) to embarrassed, sad, or mad. Ask for students to share examples of teasing and write these on chart paper.

2. Ask students to think about why people tease others. Write these reasons on another piece of chart paper and number these. Most often the first reason people give is that people tease others because they don't like them. This thought creates those hurt feelings of sad and mad. Help the students to realize the various other reasons that people tease that may have nothing to do with them. Include the following reasons on your list: for attention, to fit in or belong, for power or to control, for a false sense of feeling that they are better, for revenge, because they see older kids teasing and they think they are supposed to do it. Explain that so many of the reasons people tease have nothing personal to do with the person being teased.

3. Review the two lists on chart paper – examples of teasing and reasons why people tease – and see if the group can match a possible reason for teasing by each example given. You may simply place the number of the reason by the example.

4. **Closure:** Ask: *If you were being teased and you stopped to realize that it may not have anything to do with you but there may be other reasons why they are teasing, do you think it may help you manage your feelings about it better?* Challenge students to be more aware of the reasons behind the teasing.

ACTIVITY A3.2
Don't Bite the Hook

PURPOSE: To provide strategies and practice for appropriately handling teasing and put downs.

MATERIALS NEEDED:
- Cut out activity sheets: "Free Fish" and "Hooks." Tape a large paper clip to the mouth the blank fish.
- Pole and yarn for a fishing pole – add a clothespin at the end of the yarn. Tape a magnet to the clothespin.
- Optional: *Simon's Hook* by Karen Burnett

PROCEDURE:
1. **Introduction:** Ask students if anyone has ever made fun of them by teasing or saying something mean. Give students the opportunity to share teasing they may have experienced (caution them not to share the name of the teaser in group but only to tell about what happened.) Ask students how they usually feel when they are teased – mad, sad, embarrassed, hurt? Share with them that today they are going to learn some skills for handling teasing from others that will help them feel less mad, sad, embarrassed, or hurt.

2. If you are choosing to read the storybook *Simon's Hook* by Karen Burnett, introduce and read the story at this time. If you are not reading the story you can summarize the story by asking if any of them have ever been fishing before. Discuss the concept of fishing with the fisherman using the hook with bait to "tease" the fish and to try to catch them. Point out that there are times when the fish aren't biting and it seems the fish are too smart to bite and just stay away and remain free fish. Relate fishing to teasing. The people that tease us are like the fisherman and when teasing happens we don't need to bite the hook – to fall for or react to their teasing – but, we need to leave and stay away to be a free fish/person.

3. Display the fish marked as "Be a Free Fish... Leave or Stay Away." Discuss how this strategy can be used to handle teasing. Display the other fish as you discuss the following strategies: don't react – do little or nothing, laugh or make a joke, distract or change the subject, get busy doing something else, agree with them. Give examples for each and add other strategies of your own on the blank fish given.

4. Bring out the fishing pole and take turns adding different hooks (see hook activity sheet) to the clothespin. Have the students choose which free fish (see free fish activity sheet) they would use to handle the specific hooks or teasing. Continue to entice them with your hook on the fishing pole adding more to the teasing. But as they continue to hold their own, respond with, "I guess you're just too smart to fall for the teasing." If the student responds to the teasing inappropriately, hand him/her a blank fish and pretend to get caught. Discuss with them why what they said would get them caught. Allow them to try again choosing a free fish.

continued

5. Process how students feel when they are using the positive strategies to handle teasing.

6. **Closure:** Challenge the students to continue using the positive strategies for handling teasing so they can remain free.

Ask the students to take home a letter to their parent/teacher sharing the information that they learned today. Encourage them to explain the activity to the adult and ask their help to encourage them to use these strategies. Share with them that a summary of the strategies for handling teasing have been included on a free fish at the bottom of the note. Suggest to the student that after the adult has read the letter, cut out and display the free fish somewhere to remind them of the strategies – perhaps on the refrigerator, in a notebook, on a bulletin board, etc.

Free Fish Activity Sheet

Directions: To set up, copy and cut the fish and hooks on the following pages. On the blank fish with no words, tape a large paper clip to the mouth. Make a fishing pole from a stick/pole and yarn/string — add a clothespin to the end of the yarn/string and tape a magnet to the clothespin.

To Play: Add different hooks to the fishing pole and have students take turns choosing their free fish and responding accordingly. Use the "Be a Free Fish and…" for students to create their own appropriate ways to deal with teasing. If a student responds to the teasing in an inappropriate way, hand them a blank fish and pretend to get caught. Discuss with them why what they said would get them caught. Allow them to try again choosing a free fish.

Free Fish Activity Sheet

Be a FREE Fish...
Distract or change
the subject.

Be a FREE Fish...
Laugh or make
a joke.

Be a FREE Fish
and...

Free Fish Activity Sheet

Be a FREE Fish...
Get busy doing
something else.

Be a FREE Fish...
Agree with them.

Hook Activity Sheet

Hook Activity Sheet

PARENT/TEACHER NOTE
Don't Bite The Hook Activity

Dear Parent/Teacher,

Today in group we talked about positive ways for handling teasing. So often we feel mad, hurt, or embarrassed when others are teasing us or saying mean things. We cannot control what others say to us, but we can still control how we choose to handle ourselves. We related teasing to fishing. Just as the fisherman puts his fishing line and hook in the water to tease and hook the fish, there may be some people who say mean things to try to tease and hook you into being upset. Just as in fishing there are some fish that don't bite and stay free fish. We talked about how to handle the teasing and 'not to bite' so we could stay free people.

The positive strategies we talked about are listed inside the fish below. Ask your child to explain the strategies and to give examples. Encourage your child to use these strategies in real life so he/she does not get caught by the teasing. Decide on a place to display this fish to remind you of these strategies.

Thank you for your support as we work together.

Sincerely,

Your Child's Counselor

- **Leave or Stay Away**
- **Distract or Change the Subject**
- **Laugh or Make a Joke**
- **Don't React – do little or nothing**
- **Get Busy Doing Something Else**
- **Agree with Them**

ACTIVITY A4.1
Not Included

PURPOSE: To develop coping skills to handle negative feelings when being left out.

MATERIALS NEEDED:
- Copy and cut apart the self-talk message cards on the Not Included Activity Sheet
- Copy the Not Included Thought Bubble Activity Sheet and laminate – one for each student. Cut out the strips of problem situations from the sheet.
- Erasable markers for each student.

PROCEDURE:

1. **Introduction:** Ask - *Who has ever been left out of something that your friends were doing? How does it feel?* Let students know that being left out happens to all of us at times so we need to learn how to deal with it. Ask for any suggestions.

2. Introduce the concept of self-talk. Explain self-talk as the messages we think in our heads about a situation. It is these messages that affect how we feel about a situation. Share with the students that rather than let it bother us that we were not included we need to use our positive self-talk messages. Have students choose and read the different self talk message cards from the Not Included Activity Sheet and ask the students to tell whether they are a positive or negative message.

3. Ask students if they ever like reading cartoons. Ask how the cartoon shows the thoughts of the cartoon characters. Ellicit the response of thought bubbles.

4. Give each student an enlarged thought bubble and an erasable marker. Also give each student a paper strip of a situation from the Not Included Thought Bubble Activity Sheet describing a time a person was left out. Have them write a positive self talk statement on their bubble that they could use to help them deal with the situation. When they share their situation and self talk statement with the group let them hold their bubble beside their head as in a cartoon.

5. **Closure:** Encourage students to use the self-talk messages to help them in real life situations.

Not Included Activity Sheet

Directions: Copy and cut apart the cards. Read each and decide if the self talk statement is a positive or negative message.

Situation: Not getting invited to a classmate's birthday party.
Self-Talk: Nobody likes me. I'm no good.

Situation: Not getting invited to a classmate's birthday party.
Self-Talk: Oh well – I'll find something else to do.

Situation: You did not get chosen for the baseball team.
Self-Talk: I'll never get anything that I try for.

Situation: You did not get chosen for the tennis team.
Self-Talk: I may not be good enough for the team, but I can still enjoy tennis.

Situation: You did not get chosen for the baseball team.
Self-Talk: I do not have to be the best at everything I try.

Situation: The teacher did not call on you to answer the question even though you raised your hand.
Self-Talk: The teacher doesn't like me, that's why she won't call on me.

Situation: The teacher did not call on you to answer the question even though you raised your hand.
Self-Talk: That's okay. She has to give others a turn to answer.

Situation: Nancy chose Shelby to be in her group instead of me.
Self-Talk: Nancy likes Shelby better than me! I'll show her – I just won't talk to her anymore.

Situation: Nancy chose Shelby to be in her group instead of me.
Self-Talk: That's okay. This will give me a chance to be in a different group and get to know someone else better.

Not Included Thought Bubble Activity Sheet

What would be a positive self-talk message if you didn't get voted by your class to be on student council?
What would be a positive self-talk message if you didn't get picked for the kick-ball team?
What would be a positive self-talk message if you didn't get invited to the neighborhood party?
What would be a positive self-talk message if your friends didn't save you a place at lunch?
What would be a positive self-talk message if your friends wouldn't let you play with them at recess?
What would be a positive self talk message if your best friend chose someone else to be their partner?

ACTIVITY A5.1
Trouble Learning Something New

PURPOSE: To help students cope with difficult tasks.

MATERIALS NEEDED:
• Trouble Learning Something New Activity Sheet copied for each student.

PROCEDURE:

1. **Introduction:** Ask: *Who in here has ever had trouble learning something new? Maybe you didn't get it the first, second, or third time and you felt like quitting. How do you feel when that happens?*

2. Ask how many know how to walk? Were you born knowing that or did you have to learn it? They probably don't recall their own experience in learning how to walk but ask them to relate the typical experience with learning to walk with all of the falling down and getting up, the wobbly steps, and then improvement with practice. Point out that people learn to walk at different ages but once they learn how to walk there is no way to tell who learned first, second, third, etc. Propose a "what if." What if a baby gets mad when he/she keeps falling down in learning to walk and just quits and gives up and does not try anymore? It would seem a little strange if you were your age and still crawling around because you didn't know how to walk. Relate the same type of questions to learning how to ride a bike without training wheels. Ask them if they agree or disagree with the statement that all through life they will continually be faced with situations that are hard or difficult. Share that when we have these difficult situations we have a choice to get upset and feel miserable or to keep a positive thought about it and keep trying.

3. Ask the students advice on what you tell yourself or do when you come across something that is hard to do or difficult to learn. Relate it to the advice of a coach encouraging his team to play their best.

4. Have students complete and share the Trouble Learning Something New Activity Sheet.

5. **Closure:** Encourage students to make the choice not to get mad or frustrated but to carry a coach up in their heads to give them advice on trying their best.

Trouble Learning Something New
Activity Sheet

Directions: Choose one thing that you are trying now to learn that may be challenging or difficult for you. Write it on the lines below. Next think of encouraging words a coach might say to help you cope and do your best with this difficult task. Write this information inside the coach's talk bubble.

SITUATION:

ACTIVITY A5.2
It's Okay to Make Mistakes

PURPOSE: To understand that mistakes happen and to learn to deal with them in a positive way.

MATERIALS NEEDED:
• Write or type out one per page the famous quotes given in procedure step 2.
• Copy and cut apart the cards from the It's Okay to Make Mistakes Activity Sheet
• Index cards and pencils for each student

PROCEDURE:
1. **Introduction:** Ask the students if they have ever called their teacher "mom"? Or got on the wrong bus to go home? Or forgot to put their name on their paper? Or completed the wrong assignment for homework? Point out that these are mistakes people make. Define a mistake as something said or done that unintentionally/accidentally turned out to be wrong. Ask students how people may feel when they make a mistake - embarrassed, sad, mad?

2. Introduce famous sayings about mistakes. Ask the students to explain what they think the sayings mean. Display the quotes.
   • He who is afraid to make mistakes is afraid to succeed. (Thomas Edison)
   • The only man who never makes a mistake is the man who never does anything. (Theodore Roosevelt)
   • A life spent in making mistakes is not only more honorable but more useful than a life spent in doing nothing. (George Bernard Shaw)
   • Success in the end eclipses the mistakes along the way. (Chinese Proverb)
   • Mistakes are okay as long as you learn from them. (add your name here)

3. Complete the It's Okay to Make Mistakes Activity Sheet.

4. Distribute to the students a blank index card and have them write on the card their advice to others about helpful ways to handle or to think about making mistakes. Collect these cards and type each person's name and their advice on a sheet entitled "Famous Quotes on Helpful Ways to Handle Mistakes" and hand out to the students on their next visit.

5. **Closure:** Summarize that everyone makes mistakes and mistakes are okay as long as you learn from them and keep a positive attitude about making mistakes.

It's Okay to Make Mistakes Activity Sheet

Directions: Copy and cut apart the following statements. Pass out the cards to the students and have the students take turns reading the cards and telling whether it is True if the statement is a helpful way to deal with mistakes and False if it is not. Explain why or why not. Discuss how you might feel if you were thinking that way.

That was so dumb of me to make that mistake! Why did I do it?	**The mistake was an accident and accidents happen.**	**Everyone makes mistakes sometimes. At least I'm "normal."**
Continue to think about how awful that mistake was for days.	**Apologize if the mistake hurt someone else.**	**Blame the mistake on someone else.**
Get mad and take it out on someone else.	**Correct the mistake and try again.**	**Go off and pout about your mistake.**
Figure out what you can learn from the mistake.	**If it was a funny mistake and it didn't hurt anyone, laugh about it!**	**Give up and never try that activity again.**

ACTIVITY A6.1
In Trouble

PURPOSE: To help students handle corrections in a positive way.

MATERIALS NEEDED:
- Blank paper, pencils, crayons for each student
- In Trouble Activity Sheet copied and cut apart.
- Picture of the stop sign and the brain from the In Trouble Picture Sheet. Place these pictures in a bag.

PROCEDURE:

1. **Introduction:** Ask: *Have you ever been in trouble? What usually happens?*

2. Hand each student a sheet of paper and have them fold the paper in half diagonally. Ask them to draw/color in the top triangle a picture of what usually happens when they get in trouble at home? In the bottom triangle have them draw/color a picture of what happens when they get in trouble at school? Allow students to share their pictures and discuss. Follow up with additional questions for the group:
   - Do you lose your temper when you get corrected for doing something wrong? What happens then? How do you feel when you get in trouble for losing your temper – even madder, scared, guilty, lonely?
   - How do you wish you could handle it when you get corrected at home? At school?
   Summarize that making wrong choices sometimes and getting into trouble happens to all of us but that if we want to grow to be our best we have to be willing to listen to the corrections and learn from what we did wrong.

3. Hold up the closed bag prepared before group and tell the students that inside this bag are some items that can help handle corrections in a positive way. The only problem is that you lost the directions telling how each item can help and you need their help to figure it out. Pull out the first item – a stop sign and ask what they think it may have to do with handling corrections well. Come to the conclusion that when we are being corrected we need to STOP, don't just react but stop and listen. Next pull out of the bag the picture of the brain. Once again discuss. Summarize that the brain reminds us to not just react but to think and respond. Share this guideline for students to consider: If an adult (person in authority) goes to the trouble of correcting you there must be something there, so stop and listen. Agree and try to improve. If you disagree with the correction wait until later and discuss in a respectful way when you are calm and in control.

4. Share with the students that the key to handling corrections well is in how we choose to think about them. Introduce the terms rational and irrational thinking. Define rational thinking as reasonable, logical thinking that is true as opposed to irrational thinking which is based on false beliefs of illogical thinking. Rational thinking is important in handling corrections well. Follow the directions on the In Trouble Activity Sheet to review and discuss these different thoughts.

5. **Closure:** Tell students to remember the stop sign and the brain to help them with handling corrections.

In Trouble Picture Sheet

In Trouble Activity Sheet

Directions: Copy and cut out the cards. Select a card, read, and decide whether the statement is a TRUE (a rational, reasonable, or logical) way of thinking or a FALSE (an irrational or illogical) way of thinking. Have students explain their answer. Emphasize the importance of rational, logical and reasonable thinking in helping to deal with problems.

When I accept a correction from a teacher or parent it means that I did something wrong and I must be a bad person because of the wrong I did.	**If I deny it then they don't know for sure I did it and they won't give me a negative consequence.**	**If I blame my mistakes on others then it will create an additional problem so I better not.**
I need to listen to the correction and learn from it so I can do better.	**All people make mistakes or wrong choices some-times but the biggest mistake would be not learning from the correction.**	**I need to accept responsibility for my actions.**

ACTIVITY A7.1
That's Not Fair!

PURPOSE: To learn how to cope when you feel things are not fair.

MATERIALS NEEDED:
- Chart paper and marker
- 2 puppets preferably with moveable mouths
- That's Not Fair! Activity Sheet – a copy for each pair of students

PROCEDURE:

1. **Introduction:** Ask: *How many of us have ever said "That's Not Fair!"?* Give an opportunity for students to share stories and discuss. Introduce two puppet friends as "Our Super Heroes" who, with the students' help, can help us find respectful, positive ways to deal with situations when we think things are not fair.

2. Have students brainstorm a list of typical situations in which they feel things are unfair and write these on chart paper. On a second column on the chart paper brainstorm positive suggestions on what to THINK, SAY and DO to handle the situation well. On the list include: realize that people have different perspectives on what is fair and not; fair does not necessarily mean equal amounts but meeting what your needs are; life's not fair – deal with it because it's not worth getting upset over every small thing; if it is something major that you need to address, do it in a respectful way such as using an "I" message.

3. Do a role play activity by pairing up students and having each pair choose one of the unfair situations listed on the newsprint. Their assignment is to work out a role play based on the unfair situation. The second part of their role play needs to include the two super hero puppets that talk about good ways to think about and deal with the unfair situation. Give each pair a That's Not Fair! Activity Sheet to provide a guideline for them to write out their script. Allow time to work on these projects and then have the students perform their role play for the group.

4. **Closure:** Encourage the students to carry their Super Hero in their head in order to help them deal well with unfair situations.

That's Not Fair! Activity Sheet

Directions: Partner the group and have each pair choose an unfair situation to role play. The second half of the role play needs to include a Super Hero who comes to the rescue with good advice on how to stay calm and handle what they feel is an unfair situation. Use the lines below to write out ideas for the script.

Unfair Situation: _____

_____

_____

_____

_____

Super Hero to the Rescue! (Add thoughts and suggestions to stay calm and to handle the unfair

situation in a positive way) _____

_____

_____

_____

_____

_____

ACTIVITY A8.1
Weighted Down with Problems

PURPOSE: To encourage students to deal with their problems effectively in order to maintain positive mental health.

MATERIALS NEEDED:
- A book bag
- 4 or 5 large, medium weight rocks
- Small pebbles for each group member

PROCEDURE:

1. **Introduction:** Ask: *Have you ever felt like you were having one problem after another and they were just building up inside? For example you get yelled at by your parent, get into a fight with your brother, and your friend gets mad at you. How does it feel? Is it difficult to handle day-to-day stuff when other problems are bothering you?*

2. Pull out an empty book bag. Ask a group member to hold it or put it on their back. Ask them if they felt like they could go about their day doing what needs to be done while carrying this bag with them. Next add a heavy rock. As the rock is added tell the group that this stands for a problem that comes up in your day that is not resolved or managed. Ask for suggestions from the group as to the type of problem it could be and assign a problem to the rock. Explain that if this problem is not dealt with it won't go away. Ask a different student to hold or put the bag on their back now. Ask if it would be comfortable to go about their day carrying the bag now. Add additional problem rocks involving different students and asking the question - would it be comfortable to go about your day carrying this heavy load? End the sequence of adding rocks with the questions: *Would it be easy to run and play at recess with this book bag, to eat lunch with it, to participate in PE with it? Do you think we would be in a good mood if we had this to carry around all the time? Do you think we might get mad more easily when we carry around this heavy load? What do you think we need to do with these rocks?* Point out that when we have problems we need to deal with them in order to get rid of the problems and shrink them down to size. At this point go through the process of removing the rocks from the bag, naming the problem again and then talking about ways to deal with the problem effectively in order to get rid of it. Include such suggestions as: *Talk to someone you trust about the problem, choose to think about the problem in a better way, do something about the problem that can make it better, write it down in a journal, tell it to your pet or stuffed animal, sort it out in your head, choose to let the problem go, etc.*

3. Ask the students to think of a problem that they may have had recently that they were carrying around with them. As each student takes a turn to share that problem let them hold a large rock. Next have them tell how they could get rid of the problem or shrink the rock – exchange their large rock for a small pebble. Allow them to take their pebble with them.

4. **Closure:** Encourage them to use their pebble to remind them to deal with and shrink their problems so their problems don't weigh them down.

ACTIVITY A8.2
Stretched and Stressed by Problems

PURPOSE: To provide skills/strategies to alleviate stress.

MATERIALS NEEDED:
- Large rubber band
- Chart paper and marker

PROCEDURE:

1. **Introduction:** Hold a rubber band in front of the group and begin to stretch it little by little. As you stretch further, show body language with grimace and shying away of your face. Watch to see the reaction of the group. Ask the group what would happen if you kept stretching the rubber band – it would snap! Relate the stretching of the rubber band to stress in our lives. Ask: *How do we feel when we are stressed? Do we get angry more easily?*

2. Make a list of things that may be stressful in our lives. Include: getting a bad grade, over extended with activities and work, friendship problems, parents/family not getting along. Describe that there are two types of stress – stress that comes from OUTSIDE you, for example: losing a race, being picked on, getting a bad grade, etc. The other type comes from INSIDE you (from your feelings you choose to have). INSIDE stress includes: being angry with a friend, feeling guilty for something wrong you did, sad because a friend moved, or afraid of the neighbor's dog.

3. Describe signs of stress and the reaction of the body to stress. Include: body becomes tense, headaches, stomach aches, heart pounds faster, worry and fret, feeling very tired, trouble concentrating, and not playing and doing as much as usual.

4. Discuss ways to deal, cope, and adjust to stress in a positive way. Include: exercise (do sit-ups, run, dance, sing, and shout), slow deep breaths, close the eyes and relax the body – think of a relaxing scene, use positive thinking to deal with the problems, problem solving techniques, eat healthy, and get a good night's sleep.

5. **Closure:** Stretch the rubber band out but this time bring the rubber band in as you call on a student to name a strategy to relieving stress. Stretch it out again but give another strategy as you bring it back. Point out that stress is part of our lives and we need to take care of ourselves so we don't snap!

ACTIVITY A9.1
TV Influences

PURPOSE: To create an awareness of the influence of TV and to encourage using good judgment in watching only non-violent shows.

MATERIALS NEEDED:
• TV Influences Activity Sheet copied for each student

PROCEDURE:
1. **Introduction:** Ask the students to share their favorite TV shows. Ask if they have violence in the shows – is so, what kind of violence? Discuss. In the discussion bring out how students before have said that they watch violence on TV but that they don't think it affects them – they don't pay any attention to it…

2. Ask if they think that most people watch TV just to see the commercials. Do you leave and get a snack during commercials or turn and do something else like bug your brother or sister? Do you agree that you are probably not paying your best attention to commercials?

3. Say: *See if you can complete the following sentences.* (Choose some popular commercials of the times and begin the saying and have them complete the sentence. It may surprise you how well they know something that they say they don't really listen to). Some examples may be:
   • Skittles®. Taste the (rainbow).
   • Do the (Dew).
   • Nike®. Just (do it).
   Compliment them on knowing something that they said they really don't pay any attention to. Point out that even though they may say that they are not affected by the violence on TV it is a fact that what you see and hear does become a part of you even if you don't intend it to.

4. **Closure:** Encourage students to use good judgment when watching TV. Ask them to monitor and set a goal to reduce the watching of shows with violence in them. Distribute the TV Influence Activity Sheet and review how to keep the chart during the week. Encourage them to assess their chart at the end of the week and consider making changes in their viewing habits if needed.

TV Influences Activity Sheet

Directions: Keep track of your TV shows that you watch this week and rate the violence in the shows. Mark 4 if there is **a lot** of violence, 3 if there is **some** violence, 2 if there is **a little** violence, and 1 if there is **none.**

Review your chart at the end of the week, assess the degree of violence in those shows, and consider making future changes in the TV shows you watch if needed.

DAY OF THE WEEK	TELEVISION SHOW WATCHED	A LOT OF VIOLENCE	SOME VIOLENCE	A LITTLE VIOLENCE	NO VIOLENCE
SUNDAY		4	3	2	1
		4	3	2	1
		4	3	2	1
MONDAY		4	3	2	1
		4	3	2	1
		4	3	2	1
TUESDAY		4	3	2	1
		4	3	2	1
		4	3	2	1
WEDNESDAY		4	3	2	1
		4	3	2	1
		4	3	2	1
THURSDAY		4	3	2	1
		4	3	2	1
		4	3	2	1
FRIDAY		4	3	2	1
		4	3	2	1
		4	3	2	1
SATURDAY		4	3	2	1
		4	3	2	1
		4	3	2	1

ACTIVITY A9.2
Other's Influences

PURPOSE: To develop an awareness of how other people's behavior can influence our own.

MATERIALS NEEDED:
• Chart paper and markers
• Paper and pencils for each student

PROCEDURE:

1. **Introduction:** Say: *No one's perfect but on paper we can be.* I need your help to draw a body outline so we can create a person who handles their anger in an ideal way. Using chart paper have a student volunteer to lay flat on the paper, draw his/her outline and then display the paper for the group. Ask the group to share good qualities or actions to create the perfect person in handling problems. With a marker add this information to the paper. For example: by the head add "thinking brain"; by the mouth, "Use regular words and regular voice to handle problems"; heart – "kindness of heart"; ears – "willing to listen to the other side of the story"; hands/feet – "using peaceful/calm ways to handle, etc".

2. Tell the students to think about the people in their life and rate them on how well they feel they handle their anger when problems arise. On chart paper write down general groups of people for them to rate such as: teachers, parents, brother/sister, friends, classmates. Write the rating scale with 5 standing for handling their anger GREAT, 4 GOOD, 3 OKAY, 2 NOT SO GOOD, 1 POOR. Hand out a sheet of paper to each student and ask them to write down the names and ratings. Let them know that they do not need to share this information with the group and you will be collecting the papers at the end. Share that the ratings will give them a chance to review how other people's behavior may be influencing them.

3. When they have completed the ratings, ask the students to review their sheet to determine whose behavior shows positive ways of handling their anger in which they may want to copy or imitate that behavior. If someone on their list does not handle anger well then that would be a behavior they would not want to imitate. Caution that all people are good but we all have strengths and weaknesses and we want to look to people's strengths to copy them in order to be our best. (If you sense that there is poor handling of anger from prominent role models in their life you may add that we cannot control it if someone else is handling their anger poorly but we can make a good choice not to also do that behavior. You may need to follow up individually).

4. At the bottom of their sheet, ask the students to write one name of someone they feel handles their anger well and place a check mark by that name. Direct them to specify good anger management skills they have seen in that person and share the skills with the group. Collect the papers.

5. **Closure:** Encourage them to look for good role models and make good choices about their behavior.

ACTIVITY A10
Anger Solutions

PURPOSE: To summarize the skills of anger management discussed in group.

MATERIALS NEEDED:
• Anger Solutions Activity sheet for each student
• Chart paper and a marker
• Pencils or pens, and scissors for each student
• Completed Anger Solutions Activity Sheet to use as an example

PROCEDURE:

1. **Introduction:** Ask students to think back and share the different strategies for handling their angry feelings that the group has focused on in the previous sessions. List these on chart paper.

2. Demonstrate for them your completed Anger Solutions. Share that you have one for them to create. First they need to choose their top eight choices of ways to handle anger from their list. Then they need to write a strategy in each of the blank inner triangles and then follow the directions to cutting and folding. (Be flexible to change the anger solutions sheet to fit your group. If you have covered a variety of sub topics then write the sub topics on the middle triangle in place of the colors and put the skill or strategy on the inner triangles.)

3. Allow the students to pair up and practice their anger solutions.

4. **Closure:** Encourage the students to save their anger solutions and use it to review or to share and help a friend.

Anger Solutions Activity Sheet

To complete the Anger Solutions, cut and fold the paper following these directions:

1. Cut out the Anger Solutions along the outside solid lines.
2. Write different strategies for appropriately dealing with anger in the 8 inside triangles.
3. Place the anger solutions paper face down on a table then fold each corner into the center.
4. Turn the paper over and again fold each corner into the center.
5. Next, fold the paper in half with the numbers on the outside. Now open and fold in half the other way.
6. Place the thumb and pointer finger of each hand under the number flaps and close so the numbers show.
7. TO USE: Pick a number. Open and close the Anger Solutions this number of times. Next, pick a color. Spell out the color by opening and closing the Anger Solutions for each letter. Finally, pick a color and open the flap to read the anger solution and give it a try!

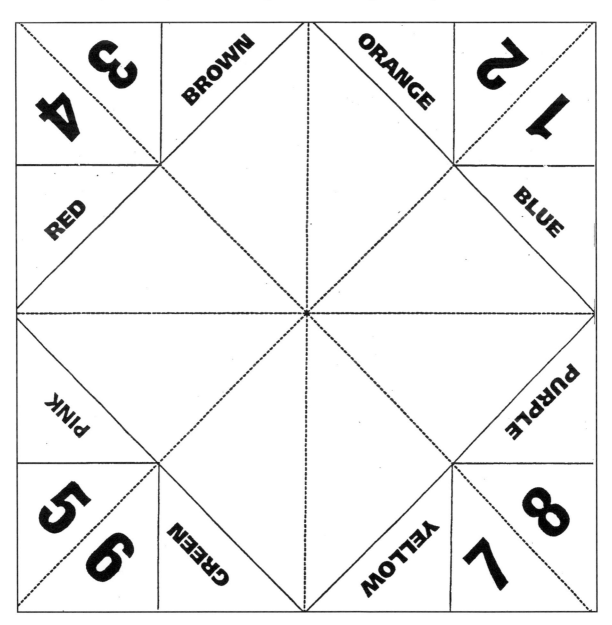

STUDENT POST ASSESSMENT FORM
Anger Management

	STRONGLY AGREE	AGREE	DISAGREE	STRONGLY DISAGREE
1. When angry I am able to use self-control. I am able to stay in control with what I say and do even though I am angry.	4	3	2	1
2. I handle disagreements with my friends well.	4	3	2	1
3. I handle being teased or picked on by others well.	4	3	2	1
4. I can handle being left out well.	4	3	2	1
5. I like how I think, feel, and act.	4	3	2	1
6. When parents or teachers correct my behavior, I handle it well.	4	3	2	1
7. When I feel things are unfair, I handle it well.	4	3	2	1
8. When I am worried about other problems I find good ways to deal with them so I can handle situations well and not have my anger get out of control.	4	3	2	1
9. I monitor what I watch on TV and the video games I play so that I am not exposed to too much violence.	4	3	2	1
10. I feel that I have participated well as a group member by listening, sharing, and learning from the group.	4	3	2	1
11. I feel that I have participated well as a group member in following through with the skills and assignments outside of the group.	4	3	2	1

12. The most helpful part of the group was:_____

13. One thing I would change about group is:_____

_____

14. Would you recommend this group to a friend? Why or why not? _____

_____

Comments:

_____

_____

_____

PARENT/TEACHER NOTE
Post Assessment

Dear Teacher/Parent,

We are concluding our small group on anger control that your child has been a participant. We have focused on the skills of:

I have enjoyed working with your child and will continue to follow up with your child during the year. To help assess the degree to which your child is implementing the skills learned, please complete the post assessment listed below and return. Your answers need to reflect your child's present behavior. Thank you.

Sincerely,

Your Child's Counselor

STUDENT/CHILD'S NAME _____

PARENT/TEACHER NEEDS ASSESSMENT

	STRONGLY AGREE	AGREE	DISAGREE	STRONGLY DISAGREE
1. When angry he/she is able to use self-control – able to stay in control with what he/she says and does even though he/she is angry.	4	3	2	1
2. He/she handles disagreements with his/her friends well.	4	3	2	1
3. He/she handles being teased or picked on by others well.	4	3	2	1
4. He/she can handle being left out well.	4	3	2	1
5. He/she likes how he/she thinks, feels, and acts.	4	3	2	1
6. When parents or teachers correct his/her behavior he/she handles it well.	4	3	2	1
7. When he/she feels things are unfair he/she handles it well.	4	3	2	1
8. When he/she is worried about other problems he/she can still handle his/her anger well.	4	3	2	1
9. He/she monitors what they watch and play on TV and video games so as not to be exposed to too much violence.	4	3	2	1
10. The people in his/her life handle their anger well.	4	3	2	1

Comments:

Friendship

Friendship

Friends and the ability to make friends is an important part of a child's development. Children need the acceptance and the support of their peers. Making and keeping friends is not as easy as one might think. First you need to learn how to connect with others and then after the initial contact more complex social skills are required to maintain a friendship. They need to learn how to be a leader as well as a follower. They need to learn how to handle rejection, how to handle peer pressure, how to be assertive to stick up for their rights, to be aware of how their behaviors can affect friendships as well as developing strategies for handling others' rude or irritating behaviors. For some children this skill development may come more natural but for others it may be more difficult. Friendship skills can be learned – it just takes time and practice.

Small group counseling offers the opportunity for students to strengthen their friendship skills. A students' friendship skill needs can vary dramatically. Some students may need help overcoming shyness and developing a comfort in talking and connecting with others. Other students may need help with reviewing their own behavior to assess if it is conducive to friendships. Others may need more help on handling typical problems that arise in friendships. Information in this book is provided for you to first assess and determine your group's specific needs and then for you to choose skill building activities from the multiple list that best meets the needs of your group. The first activity in this section 'Friendship Road' is a needs assessment activity that collects feedback from the student, teacher, and parent. Once the specific needs of your group are determined then you can use the Correlation Chart on page 133 to select session activities. The Small Group Roster and Planning Form on page 19-20 can be helpful for writing down the group plans. For each session a main skill building activity needs to be selected as well as an icebreakers/energizer chosen (See Icebreakers/Energizers Section). An additional, optional component can be added to each group session – Service Learning (See the Service Learning Section for more information).

This book is designed in hopes of helping counselors' to be focused on students' needs and to be efficient and effective in helping students.

Friendship

• INITIAL GROUP SESSION...

Review the Getting Started: First Group Sessions on page 17. Complete the Needs Assessment Activity B which includes a student and a parent/teacher needs assessment. Review the areas of need from these assessments and with the use of the Needs Assessment Correlation to Friendship Skill Building Activities Chart on page 133, plan the skill building activities for the remaining group sessions.

• SKILL BUILDING ACTIVITIES...

The following is a list of Friendship Skill building activities grouped by sub topics that relate to the needs assessment. Each activity will take about 20-25 minutes, therefore only one activity needs to be planned for each group meeting. Not all activities will be used, only those that relate to the needs of your group. Select your activities, guided by your Needs Assessment Correlation to Skill Building Activities Chart on page 133. You may also want to use the Small Group Roster and Planning Chart on pages 19-20 to organize your sessions and activities.

• CLOSING GROUP SESSION...
Review the How to End: Final Group Session on page 23. Complete the Closing Group Activity B6 which includes a student and a parent/teacher post assessment. Use this information to evaluate the group and to determine follow up with individual students on continuing weaknesses.

NEEDS ASSESSMENT ACTIVITY B
Friendship Road

Purpose: To assess the friendship needs of the students.

Materials Needed:
- Cards/Bricks from the Friendship Road Activity sheet copied and cut apart
- Student Needs Assessment copied for each student
- Parent/Teacher Needs Assessment copied for each student

Procedures:
1. **Introduction:** Ask the students if any of them have ever seen the movie "The Wizard of Oz". Explain that in the movie Dorothy is stranded trying to find her way home. The directions from the Good Witch of the West are to "follow the yellow brick road" to the city of Oz where the wizard could get her home. Relate that our goal in group is to "follow the friendship brick road" to finding success with friends.

2. Hand each student a Needs Assessment Sheet and place the cards/bricks in the center of group. Share with the students that these are the friendship bricks on the road to successful friendships. Have the students take turns drawing a card/brick and reading it to the group. Group leader may assist in the reading of the information if necessary. Group leader needs to facilitate a discussion/explanation of each card/brick.

3. As the cards/bricks are discussed, direct the students to find the number on the Needs Assessment sheet and circle to what extent this relates to them. Instruct them to circle 4 if they strongly agree that they have that friendship quality, circle 3 if they agree that they have that quality, 2 if they disagree, and 1 if they strongly disagree. Let students know that you will use this information to plan the friendship activities for the group.

4. **Closure:** Encourage the students to think about their friendships with others and the skills and work that is involved with making and keeping friends. Ask them to tune in "same time, same place" as we continue talking about friendship skills.

   Explain to the students that you have a similar assessment for their parent and/or teacher to complete. Send copies with the students to give to their Parent/Teacher to complete and return. Or you may choose to put the Needs Assessment in teachers' boxes and mail to parents.

   Refer to the Needs Assessment Correlation to Friendship Skill Building Activities Chart to assist in planning group sessions. Select an appropriate skill building activity for each session depending on the needs determined from the assessment as well as group discussions and observations.

Friendship Road Activity Sheet

Directions: Copy and cut out the friendship bricks. Have students take turns selecting and reading the information on the cards/bricks that help us to be successful with friends. Discuss and allow students to complete the number on the Needs Assessment Sheet that correlates with the number card/brick.

2 To be a friend...
It's important to know how to meet new people and make new friends.

4 To be a friend...
It's important to use good friendship behaviors in getting along with others.

1 To be a friend...
It's important to be a likable person with good friendship qualities.

5 To be a friend...
It's important to to have good skills to handle friendship problems.

3 To be a friend...
It's important to be good at listening to others – not just their words but their feelings too.

Student Needs Assessment for Friendships

Name: _____

Directions: Complete the needs assessment as directed in the Friendship Road Activity. Mark your answers honestly. The information will be collected by the group leader - no specific names and their needs will be shared with the group. The group leader will use this information to plan future friendship activities of the group based on needs.

	STRONGLY AGREE	AGREE	DISAGREE	STRONGLY DISAGREE
1. I am a likable person with good friendship qualities.	4	3	2	1
2. I know how to meet new people and make new friends.	4	3	2	1
3. I am good at listening to others—not just their words, but their feelings too.	4	3	2	1
4. I use good friendship behaviors in getting along with others.	4	3	2	1
5. I have good skills to handle friendship problems.	4	3	2	1

6. What I want to learn more about friendships is:

PARENT/TEACHER NOTE
Needs Assessment

Dear Parent/Teacher,

Friends and the ability to make friends is an important part of a child's development. Children need the acceptance and the support of their peers. Making and keeping friends is not as easy as one might think. First you need to learn how to connect with others. After the initial contact, more complex social skills are required to maintain a friendship. Children need to learn how to be a leader as well as a follower. They need to learn how to handle rejection well, how to handle peer pressure, how to be assertive to stick up for their rights, how to be aware of their own behaviors that can interfere with friendships as well as handling others' rude or irritating behaviors. For some children this skill development may come naturally but for others it may be more difficult. Friendship skills can be learned - it just takes time and practice.

In order to structure our friendship small group to meet the specific needs of the group members we need your input. Review your child's behavior over the past months, complete the needs assessment given below, and return. Please feel free to add comments or to share any information that would be helpful as we begin our small group. Thank you for your input as we work together to help our students be their best.

Sincerely,

Your Child's Counselor

PARENT/TEACHER NEEDS ASSESSMENT FOR

STUDENT/CHILD'S NAME _____

	STRONGLY AGREE	AGREE	DISAGREE	STRONGLY DISAGREE
1. He/she is a likable person with good friendship qualities.	4	3	2	1
2. He/she knows how to meet new people and make new friends.	4	3	2	1
3. He/she is good at listening to others—not just their words, but their feelings too.	4	3	2	1
4. He/she uses good friendship behaviors in getting along with others.	4	3	2	1
5. He/she has good skills to handle friendship problems.	4	3	2	1

Comments:

NEEDS ASSESSMENT CORRELATION
to Friendship Skill Building Activities

Directions: Use the chart to assist in planning skill building activities for group sessions. Below is a listing of the activities as they relate to each sub topic in the needs assessment. Select an appropriate skill building activity for each session depending on the needs determined from the assessment as well as group discussions and observations. Area of needs may be indicated by a score of "1" or "2" on an item on the assessment. For an area of heavy need you may choose to plan for several sessions utilizing several skill building activities focusing on that sub topic. For lighter needs you may choose only one session choosing only one skill building activity from that sub topic. If there is no need indicated for that sub topic then do not plan to use a skill building activity from that area. Remember these skill building activities are written covering a wide range of information but the intent is for the leader to choose only the ones that fit the group's needs. All activities will not be used in a typical 6-8 session group. Note that most skill building activities for friendship are marked by the letter B indicating this section of the book, however at times a skill building activity in another section will be referenced and will be indicated by a different section letter.

NEEDS ASSESSMENT STATEMENTS

SKILL BUILDING ACTIVITIES THAT CORRELATE

1. I am a likable person with good friendship qualities.	B1.1	B1.2	A1.3			
2. I know how to meet new people and make new friends.	B2.1	B2.2	B2.3			
3. I am good at listening to others—not just their words, but their feelings too.	B3.1	B3.2				
4. I use good friendship behaviors in getting along with others.	B4.1	B4.2	B4.3	B4.4		
5. I have good skills to handle friendship problems.	B5.1	B5.2	B5.3	A2.1	A2.2	A2.3

ACTIVITY B1.1
Friendship Jewels

Purpose: To help students be aware of the friendship qualities they possess.

Materials Needed:
- Five colored stones for each student large enough for students to write a friendship word. The colored glass stones used for fish tanks work well and is inexpensive.
- Permanent fine line markers for each student
- Small bags for each student
- Chart paper/marker

Procedures:

1. **Introduction:** Ask: *Do you like yourself?* Explain to the students that to be a friend to others you must first be a friend to yourself. Encourage discussion on the meaning of being a friend to yourself.

2. Ask the students to think about the positive qualities people have that help them be a good friend to themselves and others. Write these positive qualities on a chart. Include such words as: respectful, dependable, appreciative, kind, caring, helpful, uses good judgment, cooperative, honest, sincere, brave, resourceful, neat, flexible, loyal, forgiving, careful, loving, polite, understanding, humorous, fair, cheerful, likable, etc.

3. Ask the students to review the list of words and choose the top five that are qualities that they already possess. Give each student five colored stones and a permanent marker and ask them to write a positive quality that describes them on each stone. Have each student share their "jewels". As they share these positive qualities on the stones, put the students' initials on the chart paper beside that friendship quality and circle their initials.

4. Next give each student a small bag to put their "jewels" in. On one side of the bag have them write and answer: *Things I like to do...* and on the other side of the bag have them write and answer: *Things I'm good at that I could help others with.* Allow students to share their answers with the group. Let the students know that the bag and stones is theirs to take with them to remind themselves that they are a friendship treasure of many good qualities to offer to others.

5. (Optional) Share with the students that we are continually improving ourselves and working on being our best. To help them with this concept, at each session, have each student choose an additional quality from the chart that they want to work on. Either have them put in writing or verbalize the friendship quality they choose and their plan. Put their initial by the quality they choose that week. As they return the following week let them report on their progress. If the student/group feels that the person has mastered that friendship quality, then give them an additional colored stone and marker for them to write the word on their stone to take with them. Circle their initials on the chart to indicate mastery. Continue each week as students continue to work on strengthening their friendship qualities.

6. **Closure:** Compliment students on their strong friendship qualities that they possess that they can share with others in making friends. Let them know that each and everyone is a true treasure.

ACTIVITY B1.2
Friendship Ingredients

Purpose: To review the various thoughts and actions for being a good friend.

Materials Needed:
- Small empty pizza boxes for each student. Area pizza stores may be willing to donate these unused boxes.
- Cut out circles for each student using white construction paper. Size needs to fit as the dough/crust in the pizza box.
- Red construction paper circles cut for each student – slightly smaller than the white circles
- Yellow strips of paper – 1"x3" (about 6 per student)
- Construction paper, scissors, glue, and markers
- Optional: slice of pizza for each student

Procedures:
1. **Introduction:** Ask: *Who likes pizza! Does anyone know how to make pizza? What are the basic ingredients?* Summarize the basic ingredients as the dough, the sauce, and then the cheese/toppings. Relate these three ingredients to the three basic ingredients in Friendship – friendly THOUGHTS, friendly words you SAY, and friendly things you DO.

2. Give each student an empty pizza box. Hand each a large white circle relating it to the dough of the pizza. Ask the students to write the words "Friendly Thoughts" at the top. Discuss friendly thoughts. Have the students add this information to their friendship dough. Include such information as:
   - Everyone is important
   - Being accepting of everyone
   - Don't judge others
   - Appreciating differences
   - Look for the good in everyone, etc.

3. Next hand out a smaller red circle for the friendship sauce. Ask the students to write "Friendly Words". Discuss friendly things people say. Have the students add this information to the circle. Include such words as:
   - Thank you
   - I like that idea
   - You did a great job!
   - I'm glad you're back
   - We missed you
   - I appreciate your help
   - You're good at ____
   - You're good at drawing!
   - It's good to see you
   - Thanks for coming over
   - Thanks for inviting me, etc.

4. Hand out yellow strips of paper and provide other paper for students to cut out to make different shaped toppings for their pizza. Relate this to the ingredient of "Friendly Actions". Discuss friendly things we do. Have students add this to their pieces of paper. Include such actions as: being a good listener, helping, smiling, sharing, waiting your turn, calling people by their name, etc.

5. Have students glue their friendship pizza together in their box. On the outside of the box have them write the answers to the following: List 3 things you have said lately that were friendly. List 3 things you have done lately that were friendly. Allow students to share their friendship pizza.

6. (Optional) If it is "do-able", conclude the session by serving each student a piece of pizza. They can enjoy the real pizza as they share about their "friendship pizza". As they eat, review the ingredients to being a good friend. Perhaps make a game out of it – have each student take turns summarizing something that was shared in group before they can take their next bite of pizza.

7. **Closure:** Encourage students to make an effort to use friendly thoughts, words, and actions during the week. Ask students to take the parent/teacher note home to share the friendship information.

Dear Parent/Teacher,

In Friendship Group today we talked about the basic ingredients needed in friendships. It is important to have friendly thoughts, use friendly words, and do friendly things. Our friendly thoughts included being accepting of others, not judging others, recognizing that everyone is important, and looking for the good in people. With these basic friendly thoughts our actions and words will reflect these. We can show and share our friendliness in our words by complimenting others, letting them know you missed them, and speaking to them and saying hello. Our friendly actions are shown with a smile, by sharing, taking turns, being a good listener, and helping others.

Encourage your child to become more aware of their friendly thoughts and what they say and do and to continue showing their friendliness. Point out and compliment their friendly actions towards others.

Thank you for your support as we work together.

With Smiles,

Your Child's Counselor

ACTIVITY B2.1
Connecting with Others

Purpose: To gain skills in meeting and connecting with others.

Materials Needed:
- Two paper clips
- Cards from the Connecting with Others Activity Sheet copied and cut apart
- Chart paper and marker

Procedures:

1. **Introduction:** Ask students if they have ever been in a situation where they did not know anyone – a new student in class, at a birthday party, a large family reunion. Discuss the feelings involved and how they may have handled the situation. Explain that sometimes it is hard to know what to say or do with others.

2. Hold two paper clips in your hand and share that these paper clips can be like people. Two people/paper clips can pass and keep right on going – demonstrate the paper clips passing each other but making no contact. Or the two people/paper clips can pass and with a little effort they can connect – at this point hook the paper clips together as they pass. Share that the first step to making friends is to first connect with them.

3. Place the role play / replay cards from the Connecting with Others Activity sheet in the center of group. Have a student draw a card and first act out the role play given. Then have them act out the replay on the card. Ask the group to point out the differences of the two scenes and discuss which is the better way to connect with friends. Initiate a discussion on body language and how body language is just as important as your words (…a picture is worth a thousand words). On chart paper, write down the appropriate body language for connecting with others. You may choose to add this information on a body outline such as, beside the eyes write "good eye contact" beside the mouth write "smile", add a talk bubble and add the possible things to say in meeting/greeting a person. Continue with the role play allowing each student to take a turn acting out the situations on the card and adding more information to the chart.

4. **Closure:** Summarize the connecting friendship behaviors by reviewing the replays. Challenge them to practice these behaviors during their week.

Connecting with Others Activity Sheet

Directions: Copy and cut apart the cards. Have a student select a card and act out the role play given. Then have them act out the replay on the card. Ask the group to point out the differences of the two scenes and discuss which is the better way to connect with friends.

Role Play: Come into the room with your head down and no eye contact.

Replay: Come into the room with your head up, pleasant look on your face and good eye contact.

Role Play: Come into the room with an angry look on your face, stomping, and sitting down in the seat making lots of noise.

Replay: Come into the room with a smile on the face and join the group.

Role Play: Come in the room and pull a seat away from the group and sit down by yourself.

Replay: Come in the room and sit down in a chair with the group. Have a pleasant look on your face with good eye contact.

Role Play: Come into the room with your arms folded and a pout on your face.

Replay: Come into the room with your hands beside your side, pleasant look on your face, and head nods if appropriate.

Role Play: Hesitate coming in the room, sit down and don't look at anyone.

Replay: Come in the room with a pleasant look, sit down next to someone and ask, "Hey, how are you?"

Role Play: Come into the room with hand up to the mouth and pretending to laugh at others.

Replay: Come into the room with hands beside your side, pleasant look on your face and good eye contact.

ACTIVITY B2.2
The Big Mouth

Purpose: To gain information on what to say to and talk about with others to get to know them.

Materials Needed:
• Big Mouth Activity sheet for each student
• Pencils/pens

Procedures:

1. **Introduction:** Ask: *In meeting a new person, what do you say after 'Hi'?* Discuss. Explain to students that in talking with students you are trying to find things that you have in common. Asking questions about things you like is a good way to find out if they like the same things.

2. Hand each student a Big Mouth Activity sheet. Explain to them that inside the mouth they are to write questions to ask or things to talk about with someone else in order to get to know them and to find out what things you may have in common. You may choose to set it up as a contest giving five minutes to see who can come up with the most information. Have students share their information allowing others to add to their sheet any new information shared.

3. Ask each student to select someone that they would like to meet or to get to know better. Have them devise a plan of when, where, how, and what they will say. Have the students put their plan in writing on the bottom of the Big Mouth Activity sheet.

4. Have students pair up and take turns role playing meeting the person they want to get to know. After the role play, predict the positive and negative outcomes of how this meeting could go in real life. Positive – could connect with and make a new friend; negative – they could ignore you and not answer. Discuss how you could handle the negative outcome. Tell students to not get discouraged if it does not work. Encourage them to select another person they would like to try to get to know, smile, and try again.

5. **Closure:** Assign their homework to implement their plan of talking with their selected student. Make sure to allow students at the beginning of the next session to report on how this experience went.

Big Mouth Activity Sheet

Directions: Inside the picture of the mouth, write questions or things to talk about with someone else in order to get to know them. Find out things you may have in common.

The Plan...

Who: The person I would like to get to know better is:
_____.

What to say: _____
_____

When: _____.

Where: _____.

ACTIVITY B2.3
Speaking Up!

Purpose: To help students overcome shyness and gain the courage to talk to others.

Materials Needed:
• Speaking Up! Activity sheet for each student
• Plain paper and pencils/crayons/markers for each student

Procedures:

1. **Introduction:** Ask students if they have ever been shy about speaking to others. Allow students to share. Explore the thoughts behind this shyness. Include such thoughts as: not knowing what to say, afraid to say the wrong thing, worried about being embarrassed, worried the other person may not listen or respond well, etc.

2. Explore the concept of "self talk". Ask them to explain what a pep talk is or relate it to that of a coach talking to encourage his/her team to do well. Have a volunteer pretend to be the coach giving a pep talk to you about going up and talking to someone you don't know.

3. Explain the importance of the thoughts in your head. The positive thoughts in your head can be like the pep talk given by the coach. Distribute the Speaking Up! Activity sheet. Take turns having students point out the positive helpful brain thoughts and discuss. As they share, tell the students to circle the positive statements. Review the negative statements and discuss why those statements would not be helpful.

4. Give each student a sheet of paper. Assign the following scenarios, one to each student, and have them write it at the top of their paper:
   • in a store when the salesclerk gives you the wrong change
   • taking cookies over to a new neighbor who has just moved in
   • talking to your teacher about an incorrect grade on a paper
   • speaking to the new student who just joined the class
   • you are the new student in class meeting others
   • you are at a party where you don't know many people
   Instruct the students to draw cartoons and to write in the talk bubbles the things they may say to others in the situation given to them.

5. **Closure:** Encourage students to use their positive thoughts in their brain to initiate conversations with others. Tell them to appreciate it when they are successful connecting with someone but if it does not work – simply try again. Remember practice makes perfect.

Speaking Up! Activity Sheet

Directions: Circle the positive statements in the brain that are helpful thoughts in connecting with others.

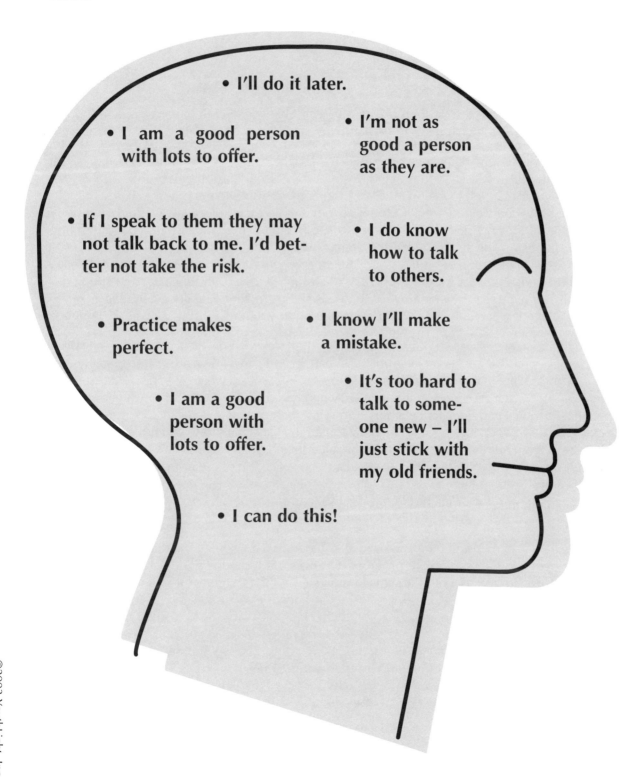

- I'll do it later.
- I am a good person with lots to offer.
- I'm not as good a person as they are.
- If I speak to them they may not talk back to me. I'd better not take the risk.
- I do know how to talk to others.
- Practice makes perfect.
- I know I'll make a mistake.
- I am a good person with lots to offer.
- It's too hard to talk to someone new – I'll just stick with my old friends.
- I can do this!

ACTIVITY B3.1
Listening Pairs... Apples, Oranges*

Purpose: To strengthen an important part of friendship – listening skills.

Materials Needed:
• whistle

Procedures:

1. **Introduction:** Share with the students one of the basic skills needed in being a good friend is to be a good listener. Ask the students to explain why listening is important.

2. Divide the students into pairs. Ask each pair to designate one as the apple and one as the orange. Ask the apples to raise their hand. Instruct them to think of their favorite activity they like to do that they can tell to their partner in a moment. Whisper to the oranges, without apples hearing, that they are to ignore their partner as they talk to them – look away, fiddle with their shoes, turn around, yawn, etc. Instruct the apples to begin talking to their partners. After a brief time have them stop and process what the oranges were doing – discuss how it felt. Ask: *Have ever been ignored before? Does is feel good? Is ignoring someone a friendly thing to do?* Discuss that good listening involves good eye contact, body turned toward the speaker, and sitting quietly. Replay the same scene again however oranges are instructed to be good listeners this time. Discuss how it felt when someone was really listening to you and ask if there was a difference.

3. Next assign the oranges to talk about a favorite place they like to go on vacation. Before they begin talking, whisper to the apples to interrupt their partner with their own story immediately after oranges begin talking. After a brief time, have them stop and process what the apples did. Ask: *How did it feel?* Once again review good listening skills and add that when a friend is telling a story, it's important to be quiet and listen to the whole story. During the listening you can add head nods and "uh-uhs" and then, when they have finished say something back that shows you listened. You could summarize or ask a question. Let them know that after they have been good listeners then they can share their own story. Replay the same scene again, however apples are instructed to be good listeners this time – instruct them to use all of the skills of good listening – eye contact, sitting quietly, body turned toward the talker, head nods, uh-uhs, and say something back that shows you were listening. Discuss how the good listening felt and ask if there was a difference.

4. For the final exchange, instruct the apples to talk in detail about something that they did recently that they feel good about and are proud of. Oranges are to be the good listeners. Explain to them that apples are to talk until the whistle blows but when they hear that whistle they need to stop talking immediately. Oranges are to repeat back the last three words they heard their partner say. Allow time for the activity and the checking of words. Switch roles and repeat the activity. Facilitate a discussion of the activity focusing on what skills it took to be able to repeat the last three words. Include that good listening takes energy, concentration, and a focus on the speaker rather than on the next thing the listener wants to say.

5. **Closure:** Challenge students to practice good listening skills with their family and friends.

*adapted with permission from Senn and Sitsch (1996). Coping with Conflict. Chapin, SC: YouthLight, Inc.

ACTIVITY B 3.2
Feelings Behind the Words

Purpose: To encourage the importance of listening for the feelings behind the words in order to connect with others.

Materials Needed:
- Statement and Feeling Cards copied and cut apart from the Feelings Behind the Words Activity sheet
- Chart paper and marker

Procedures:

1. **Introduction:** Have a pair of students stand back to back in front of the group. Ask them to think about how they might feel in the following situation and make that feeling face. Use situations that may have mixed feelings like: seeing a snake, or how you felt about first learning to swim, or how you feel about major roller coasters, etc. Let the group discuss how each student was feeling. Point out that it is not unusual for people to have different feelings about the same situation. Come to the conclusion that we cannot assume that people feel the same way we do – ask the group how we can go about finding out how someone feels. Point out the importance of body language, facial expressions, and the sound in the voice. Propose the following situation: a person insists on she and her friend playing with a pet snake even though the friend is very afraid of snakes. Ask what that may do to their friendship.

2. On chart paper write the basic feeling words under the headings "pleasant" and "unpleasant". Under "pleasant" write: happy, excited, proud, surprised. Under "unpleasant" write: angry, sad, afraid, shy. Have students demonstrate how these feelings might look.

3. Place the Statement Cards and the Feeling Cards from the Feelings Behind the Words Activity sheet in the center in group. Have a student draw one Feeling Card and one Statement Card. Instruct them to read their statement to the group reflecting in voice and body the feeling given on the Feeling Card. Let students refer to the listing of feeling words on the chart paper to guess the correct feeling. Discuss what helped them know the true feeling behind the words. Discuss what they could do next to help that friend if they were feeling that way. At some point bring into the discussion how a person might feel when their friend does and does not pick up on the feelings behind their words.

5. **Closure:** Encourage students to be more aware of their friends' feelings during the week. With this awareness comes the responsibility to respond in caring ways.

Feelings Behind the Words Activity Sheet

Directions: Copy and cut apart the Statement and Feeling Cards given below. Place the cards in separate stacks in the center of group. Have a student draw one Feeling Card and one Statement Card. Instruct them to read their statement to the group reflecting in voice and body the feeling given on the Feeling Card. Let students guess the correct feeling.

Statement	**Statement**
Statement	**Statement**
Statement	**Statement**
Statement	**Statement**

Feelings Behind the Words Activity Sheet

Who was that?	**I made the team**
What are you doing?	**Yes you can.**
I saw what you did.	**I can't wait to get there.**
I got my test back.	**Are you going to the game tonight?**

Feelings Behind the Words Activity Sheet

Feeling	**Feeling**
Feeling	**Feeling**
Feeling	**Feeling**
Feeling	**Feeling**

Feelings Behind the Words Activity Sheet

Happy	**Excited**
Proud	**Sad**
Surprised	**Afraid**
Angry	**Shy**

ACTIVITY B.4.1
The Friendship Cube

Purpose: To review and emphasize the importance of behaving in a friendly way towards others.

Materials Needed:
- Copy The Friendship Cube Activity sheet for each student
- Scissors, marker, tape
- Chart paper and marker

Procedures:
1. **Introduction:** Ask: *What if someone was not honest with you, not polite, and didn't play fairly? Would you want to play with them? Why or Why not?*

2. On chart paper talk about and list important friendly behaviors that are needed to maintain friendships. You may include such behaviors as: being honest, being polite, being fair, cooperative, forgiving, loyal, dependable, kind, understanding, a good listener, respectful, etc.

3. Give each student a Friendship Cube Activity sheet. Have the students choose their top six friendly behaviors and write them on their cube – one in each space in the three squares across the top and the center squares going down the middle. Follow the directions to cut apart the cube, fold and tape together.

4. Have students take turns rolling their cubes and explaining to the group the importance of and examples of the friendly behavior they rolled.

5. **Closure:** Encourage students to assess if they consistently display the friendly behaviors on the cube. If not, encourage them to make a plan for improvement. Ask the students to take their cube home to show and explain to their parent/teacher along with a brief note letting them know the skill learned in group.

PARENT/TEACHER NOTE
The Friendship Cube

Dear Parent/Teacher,

In our friendship group today we talked about the importance of friendly behaviors. The best way to have friends is to be a good friend to others. Each student created their own Friendship Cube listing their top six friendly behaviors. Ask your child to review their cube with you. When you see your child using a friendship behavior, compliment him/her. Perhaps take time in the evening for your child to roll the cube and have him/her point out if that friendly behavior was used during the day. If the opposite of the friendly behavior occurred have your child make a plan for improvement – "What I could have said or done differently…" Thank you for continuing to work together.

Sincerely,

Your Child's Counselor

Friendship Cube Activity Sheet

Directions: In the three squares across the top and the center squares going down write your top six friendly behaviors from the list created in the lesson. Then cut out along the dotted lines and fold along the solid lines. Fold in the shape of a cube and tape together. Use the cube to continually remind you of the importance of friendly behaviors.

ACTIVITY B4.2
Leading and Following

Purpose: To explore the responsibilities involved in being a leader and a follower with friends.

Materials Needed:
- Chart paper and marker

Procedures:

1. **Introduction:** Play the game "Train". Have students line up with you being the head of the line as the train engine and the group members as the other train cars. Students need to connect their hands to the person's waist in front. Explain to them that they are to follow the lead of the engine by copying the motions and movements of the engine. As you begin, make it difficult for them to follow: move your hands out and in, up and down very quickly, hum your own song pretending to be oblivious to anything else, as you move make quick turns that are difficult to follow, perhaps as you turn bump into the train members in the back and tell them to "get out of my way". End the game and have students return to their seats. Process what happened. Ask: *Was I good train leader? Why or Why not?* (Elicit such responses as: didn't use good manners, didn't check to see if the group could follow, didn't do things that all could do, didn't seem to pay any attention to difficulties of others, didn't speak nicely to others, etc.)

2. Make a list on chart paper of the responsibilities of a good leader. Include such information as:
   - listen well to others
   - compromise if appropriate
   - encourage others
   - give compliments
   - avoid being bossy
   - make good choices – choosing appropriate behavior and activities; etc.

3. Next make a list on chart paper of the responsibilities of a good follower. Include such information as:
   - being willing to listen to and work with the leader
   - supporting the leader
   - willingness to try things "other people's way", etc.

4. Replay the game of Train. Begin with you as leader of the train but this time be an example of a good leader. Move slower, communicating your moves well and checking on your group members to see if they are following. Give encouraging statements as to how well they are doing. After you have modeled good leadership behavior then explain that you are moving to the end to become a follower and that the next person becomes the leader. As the follower now, once again model good behavior – following the leader. Take turns until each member has had a turn leading and following.

5. Process the game including such questions as: *What did you need to think when you were the leader? the follower? How did it feel when you were the leader? the follower?* Ask them to share situations in which they have been a leader and/or a follower. Ask: *Do you think this awareness of the responsibilities of being a leader and a follower will change your future behaviors. If so, in what way?*

6. **Closure:** Encourage students to know how to be both a good follower and leader.

ACTIVITY B4.3
Watch Your Manners!

Purpose: To promote the importance of good manners in friendships.

Materials Needed:
- Copy and enlarge the good manner cartoon situations on the Watch Your Manners! Activity sheet. Laminate so these can be continually written on and erased.
- Dry erase markers for each student.

Procedures:
1. **Introduction:** Ask the four basic "W" questions about good manners: *WHAT are good manners?* (Elicit such responses as: being nice to others, polite, respectful, etc.) *WHERE should you use good manners?* (Everywhere) WHEN should you use good manners? (All the time) *WHY should you use good manners?* (Elicit such responses as to be nice to others, to get along with others, so others will like you and think/know you are nice, and because it's the right thing to do!)

2. Hand out markers and the cartoon situation cards from the Watch Your Manners! Activity sheet. Explain to the students to read the situation and write a good mannered response in the cartoon bubble. Share the responses and discuss. In the discussion bring up the Golden Rule: Do unto others as you would have them do unto you. Have students check their response on the situation card to see, if the situation were reversed, if they would appreciate the response given.

3. **Closure:** Ask: *When your friends are polite to you (for example, saying thank you and asking politely about borrowing something), do you think well of your friends? Why?* Emphasize the importance of always being at our best to use good manners.

Watch Your Manners! Activity Sheet

Directions: Copy and enlarge the following situation cartoons. Laminate for durability and reuse. Hand each student a situation cartoon card. Ask each student to read their situation and write a good mannered response in the cartoon bubble. Share answers and discuss.

SITUATION:
You think the person sitting next to you in class has taken your new pencil because you can't find it anywhere.

SITUATION:
At recess you were playing basketball and, after a close game, your team lost.

SITUATION:
You are standing with a group of friends who start saying bad things about one of your other friends.

Watch Your Manners! Activity Sheet

SITUATION:
You were supposed to meet your neighbor at 4:00 but you arrive 15 minutes late.

SITUATION:
You borrowed a friend's video game and by accident it dropped on the cement and cracked the case.

SITUATION:
You made a mistake and accused your friend of spreading a bad rumor about you. Later you found out that your friend had not been involved in that at all.

SITUATION:
Both you and your friend are trying out for the lead in the school play. It turns out that your friend got the part.

ACTIVITY B4.4
Friendship Blockers

Purpose: To be aware of our own behaviors and how they can affect friendships.

Materials Needed:
- A small ball to toss to group members
- Copies for each group member of the Creating a Good Reputation Activity Sheet

Procedures:
1. **Introduction:** Ask: *Has anyone ever had a friend treat them in a way they didn't like?* Allow sharing about the situation without sharing the names. Point out that we do not have control over how our friends treat us. However, we do have control over our own behavior and how we choose to behave can influence how our friends treat us.

2. Play the IF-THEN Game. Tell the students that you are going to share with them some situations – some IF-THEN statements – in which they need to complete the THEN part of the statement. Explain that the IF part will describe a certain behavior and they are to complete the THEN part that tells what a friend might think or do in response to that behavior. A ball will be tossed to someone to complete the first IF-THEN statement, then upon the beginning of the next statement the ball is tossed to another player for them to complete the ending of the statement. Continue until all statements are completed. Allow for discussions of each statement. The statements are as follows:

   - IF you brag about yourself THEN…
   - IF you bully and push others around THEN…
   - IF you tattle on others THEN…
     (talk about the difference between tattling and telling)
   - IF you are the class clown THEN…
   - If you are grumpy and in a bad mood a lot THEN…
   - If you are a sore loser when playing a game THEN…

   Add any additional negative statements of your own that may address the needs of the group. Next switch to the positive statements.
   - IF you share THEN…
   - IF you play well with others and include them THEN…
   - IF you give others compliments and say nice things to others THEN…
   - IF you smile at people THEN…

3. Ask the group what the word REPUTATION means. Explain that reputation is what other people think of you. A reputation can be good or bad. Your reputation depends on the actions you do over and over again. Explain to the students that IF they want a good reputation THEN they have to choose good behaviors.

continued

4. Ask the students to take a moment to think about their typical behaviors they have towards others. Have them decide which behaviors they want to continue and which behaviors they may want to change. Brainstorm together different positive reputations people have such as: friendly, caring, helpful, considerate, respectful, etc. Ask students to think about what reputation they want to have. Copy for each student the Creating a Good Reputation Activity Sheet. Have students complete the sheet as they make plans for creating a good reputation.

CREATING A GOOD REPUTATION

The REPUTATION that I want to be known for is...

_____

_____

_____

"Remember reputations are what people think of you and are created by your repeated actions."

Things I need to be THINKING of to have this reputation...

_____

_____

_____

Things I need to be SAYING to have this reputation...

_____

_____

_____

Things I need to be DOING to have this reputation...

_____

_____

_____

ACTIVITY B5.1
Handling Rejection

Purpose: To help students deal with rejection.

Materials Needed:
• Puppets
• Large popsicle sticks or strips of paper with the statements in Procedure Step 4 written on them.

Procedures:
1. **Introduction:** Ask: *Have you ever wanted to be friends with someone and the other person didn't want to be your friend?* Allow time to share specific examples without mentioning names. Ask: *How do you feel when this happens?* Explore the feelings of sad, mad, embarrassed, etc.

2. Have students volunteer to role play with puppets the different feelings and the thoughts behind the feelings when someone does not want to be their friend. In the role plays, help students understand how when we feel sad, we may think that something is wrong with us and we are no good, or when we get mad we may want to do something mean to them and get back at them, and when we are embarrassed we may be reluctant to try again. Come to the conclusion that we have to deal with our unpleasant feelings regarding the rejection so that we can feel better and move ahead.

3. Explain that the first question you need to ask yourself when you get rejected is: *Did I say or do anything wrong that wasn't helpful in connecting with friends?* If the answer is YES then you need to make some behavior changes. For example, if someone doesn't want to let you join their game because you cheat, or get angry and argue then you need to work on that behavior. If the answer is NO then work on dealing with your feelings about the rejection by thinking positive, productive thoughts.

4. Write the following statements on large popsicle sticks or strips of paper. Have the students draw a statement, read it, and explain what it means and how it may help in handling rejection. Next have the student role play with a puppet handling the rejection using the thought or saying from their statement. Encourage them to complete the role play with a happy ending.
    • I'll find something else to do.
    • They don't want to play with me but I'll keep looking and I'll find someone else to play with.
    • They may still like me but they may have other reasons why they don't want to play with me now.
    • They may have other things on their mind and may be in a bad mood so I'll just give them some space.
    • I'll keep using my good manners even if others don't.
    • This is a good learning experience for me on handling rejection.

5. **Closure:** Let students know that rejection happens to everybody. It's not what happens to you but how you handle it that counts.

ACTIVITY B5.2
Saying "NO" to Friends

Purpose: To learn when and how to say "No" to friends.

Materials Needed:
- Warning Flags and Bright Idea cards from the Saying "No" to Friends Activity sheet copied and cut apart.
- Saying "NO" to Friends Activity sheet copied for each student.

Procedures:
1. **Introduction:** Ask: *Have you ever had a friend ask you to do something that you didn't feel right about and knew was wrong?* Allow them to share without giving names. Brainstorm other situations for the age group of things kids ask other kids to do that are wrong. Include such things as:
   - lending someone your homework for them to copy
   - misbehaving with others in class
   - writing or drawing pictures on a park bench
   - gossiping about someone
   - sneaking into an R rated movie when your parents only gave you permission to go to the PG movie
   - stealing from the school store
   - smoking cigarettes
   - drinking alcohol.

   Caution them that it is important to have friends but not if the friends are encouraging us to do things that we know are not right. An important skill is to be able to think for yourself and have the courage to say "No" to things that are wrong for us.

2. The first step in handling a difficult situation is to be able to recognize when a situation is wrong. To help decide, ask yourself the following questions: *Does this break the law? Would someone in authority (teacher/parent) be mad if I did this? If the answer is "yes" then your answer should be "no".*

3. The second step in handling difficult situations is to be smart - don't get talked into something that you know is wrong. Place the warning flags from the Saying "NO" to Friends Activity sheet in the center of group. Have the students take turns selecting a flag, reading it to the group, discussing and cautioning the students not to fall for that line.

4. The third step in handling a difficult situation is to use a bright idea of what to say or do to say "NO". Place the Bright Idea cards from the Saying "NO" to Friends Activity sheet in the center of group. Have the students take turns choosing an idea, reading it and explaining the idea to the group. Have group members give examples of how or when you might use that bright idea.

5. **Closure:** Review the three steps and the importance of saying NO when friends are asking you to do something that is wrong. Ask students to explain what is meant by the following statement. "Friends are important but not at the expense of doing things that are wrong." You may choose to give students a Saying "NO" to Friends activity sheet to keep as a review. Ask students to also share the parent/teacher note with their parent/teacher.

Saying "NO" to Friends Activity Sheet

It is important to have friends but not if the friends are encouraging us to do things that we know are not right. An important skill is to be able to think for yourself and have the courage to say "No" to things that are wrong for us.

Three Steps to Handling Difficult Situations:

1. First: Be able to recognize when a situation is wrong. To help decide, ask yourself: Does this break the law? Would someone in authority (teacher/parent) get angry if I did this? If the answer is "yes" then your answer should be "no."

2. Second: Be smart – don't get talked into something you know is wrong. Be aware of the warning flags.

3. Third: Use a bright idea of what to say or do to say "NO."

Warning Flags

Come on, no one will know.

If you were my friend you would do this with me.

Saying "NO" to Friends Activity Sheet

Warning Flags

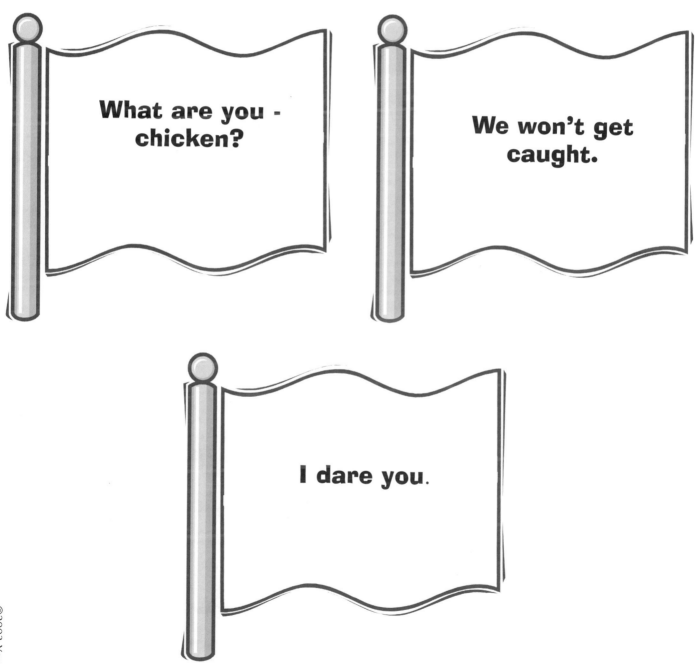

Saying "NO" to Friends Activity Sheet

Bright Ideas

Just Say No: "No way.", " That's not for me.", "I don't want to."

Make an Excuse: "I've got to go study for my test.", "I have to walk my dog."

Act Shocked: "No way!", "You've got to be crazy!"

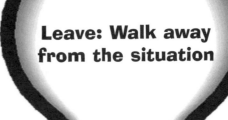

Leave: Walk away from the situation

Saying "NO" to Friends Activity Sheet

Bright Ideas

Ignore: Get busy doing something else

Better Idea: "Instead, why don't we go play basketball."

Change the Subject: "Have you seen that new movie...?"

Get Help from someone you trust.

Dear Parent/Teacher,

In friendship group today we talked about the importance of having friends but not if the friends are encouraging us to do things that we know are not right. An important skill is to be able to think for yourself and have the courage to say 'No' to things that are wrong for us. Difficult situations may come up every day for our children. A good friend may ask to borrow their homework to copy, or a group of friends may be gossiping about a classmate, or a friend may encourage your child to misbehave in class, or dare them to steal from the school store, or smoke a cigarette, or drink alcohol, etc. Our children need to be prepared to handle these pressures.

We talked about the three steps of handling a difficult situation and strategies for saying "no." Ask your child to share their Saying 'No' to Friends review sheet with you. Take time to give them some WHAT-IF situations. For example, say: "If this happens…(create a situation in which a friend may be trying to talk them into doing something wrong) … WHAT would you say or do."

I appreciate your help as we work together.

Sincerely,

Your Child's Counselor

ACTIVITY B 5.3
Dealing with Rude or Irritating Behaviors

Purpose: To increase the students' skills in dealing appropriately with rude or irritating behaviors.

Materials Needed:
- Chart paper and marker
- Create Advice Column Sheets by writing one of the following statements at the top of each sheet of paper.
  - What do you think, say, or do when someone says you are dumb?
  - What do you think, say, or do when someone takes your pencil?
  - What do you think, say, or do when someone teases you about not being able to play ball?
  - What do you think, say, or do when someone keeps tapping on their desk when you're trying to do your work?
  - What do you think, say, or do when someone brags about how they got a better grade than you did on the test?
  - What do you think, say, or do when someone teases you about your clothes?

Procedures:
1. **Introduction:** Share that all of us have experienced rude or irritating behaviors from others. Perhaps someone has teased us, said mean things to upset us, or just continues to do little things to annoy us. Allow them to share examples of rude or irritating behaviors. Ask: *What do you usually do when someone bothers you or annoys you? What do you feel like doing?* As you discuss, talk about how our first reaction when someone bothers us may be to bother them back or do something else mean. Explore how this only gets a negative cycle of "picking" going and resolves nothing. Encourage students to find appropriate ways to handle the irritating behaviors. Point out that since we cannot control others and what they choose to do then we must find an appropriate way to deal with it by our thoughts and actions.

2. Share with the students the following guideline questions to use to respond to rude and irritating behavior:
   - Will my response to the irritating behavior cause them to want to get back at me?
   - Will my response lead to other difficulties?
   - Will my response show respect for myself and others?

3. Brainstorm with the group appropriate thoughts and/or actions in responding to rude or irritating behaviors. Write these on chart paper to display. Include such strategies as: ignore them, leave, tell them how you feel (send an 'I' message), get busy doing something else, avoid them, laugh or make a joke about it, agree with them, or change the subject.

continued

4. Advice Column Activity: Tell the students that you need their help in writing an advice column for the newspaper. Distribute a pencil and an advice column sheet (prepared before group) to each student. Their job is to read the situation and then write an appropriate way they could deal with the rude or irritating behavior by their thoughts or what they could say or do. Give each student one minute to write his/her response and then call time and have them rotate the papers to the right. Then they read the next situation and write their response. Continue rotating the papers and if time allows rotate a second time. Even if the student didn't come up with a response, keep the papers moving. Let them know it's okay - they may catch it with the second time around or another group member may cover it. You may choose to give a 15 second warning each time to complete their sentence. After the activity talk about how it was hard to come up with a response that quick. Relate this to real life when you have to think fast. Share the answers from each sheet. Allow students to elaborate on their answers being shared and to add additional thoughts. Check to see if the suggestions follow the guideline questions from Step 2. Compliment the students' answers. Add additional answers if the group has more to share.

5. **Closure:** Encourage students to avoid their first response to get back at a person when someone has been rude or irritating. Instead encourage them to find an appropriate response that follows the guideline questions.

ACTIVITY B6
Friendship Stars

Purpose: To recognize friendship qualities in others and ourselves and to evaluate the group progress through post assessment.

Materials Needed:
- Friendship Stars Activity sheet for each person
- Pencils
- Student Post Assessment Form copied for each student
- Parent/Teacher Assessment Form copied for each student

Procedure:
1. **Introduction:** Ask students to review the different friendship qualities, skills, and strategies that have been discussed in the group. Share and review this information.

2. Ask them to think about each person in the group and their friendship strengths. Give examples that a person may be great at meeting new people, or a good listener, or a very caring and sensitive person, or good at handling friendship problems, or perhaps they have good manners, etc. Distribute a Friendship Star activity sheet to each student. Direct them to put their name in the center of the Star. When they are instructed to begin, they are to pass their paper to the next person on their right. That person is to look at the name on the sheet and write a friendship strength in one of the points of the stars. On the leader's cue, sheets will once again be passed to the person on their right. Continue until the papers are returned to their owners.

3. Next have each student complete the information at the bottom of the sheet. When completed have students take turns sharing this information as well as their Star information with the group.

4. Ask students to complete the Student Post Assessment Form. Allow students to share information from their forms if they choose. Send out and collect the Parent/Teacher Post Assessment.

5. Celebrate the group, the time together, what you like about everyone, and point out their successes. Encourage others to do the same.

6. **Closure:** Encourage students to appreciate and to continually work on their friendship skills for it is a lifelong process.

   Follow-Up: Follow up with students individually, consulting with their teachers, and/or sending notes to the students to encourage and compliment. Consider scheduling a monthly support group.

Friendship Star Activity Sheet

Name:

_____

The most important thing about friendships that I learned was:

_____

_____

In the future I will:

_____

_____

STUDENT POST ASSESSMENT
for Friendships

Name: _____

Directions: Complete the following post assessment reflecting your present friendship skills. Mark your answers honestly.

	STRONGLY AGREE	AGREE	DISAGREE	STRONGLY DISAGREE
1. I am a likable person with good friendship qualities.	4	3	2	1
2. I know how to meet new people and make new friends.	4	3	2	1
3. I am good at listening to others—not just their words, but their feelings too.	4	3	2	1
4. I use good friendship behaviors in getting along with others.	4	3	2	1
5. I have good skills to handle friendship problems.	4	3	2	1

6. In Friendship Group I learned: _____

_____

_____

7. The most helpful part of the group was: _____

_____

_____

8. I would recommend to change the friendship group by: _____

_____

_____

Dear Parent/Teacher,

We are concluding our small group on Friendship that your child has been a participant. We have focused on the skills of:

I have enjoyed working with your child and will continue to follow up with your child during the year. To help assess the degree to which your child is implementing the skills learned, please complete the post assessment listed below and return. Your answers need to reflect your child's present behavior. Thank you.

Sincerely,

Your Child's Counselor

PARENT/TEACHER NEEDS ASSESSMENT FOR

STUDENT/CHILD'S NAME _____

	STRONGLY AGREE	AGREE	DISAGREE	STRONGLY DISAGREE
1. He/she is a likable person with good friendship qualities.	4	3	2	1
2. He/she knows how to meet new people and make new friends.	4	3	2	1
3. He/she is good at listening to others—not just their words, but their feelings too.	4	3	2	1
4. He/she uses good friendship behaviors in getting along with others.	4	3	2	1
5. He/she has good skills to handle friendship problems.	4	3	2	1

School Success Skills

School Success

Being successful in school and building a solid academic foundation is important to future success. Utilizing the skills of listening, focusing, being organized, using time efficiently, knowing how to study, completing homework, knowing how to take tests and maintaining a good attitude are all essential skills in school success. These skills may come naturally to some children but for most of us these skills need to be taught, practiced, encouraged, structured, and maintained in order to be successful.

Small group counseling offers the opportunity for students to strengthen their skills for school success. Information in this book is provided for you to first assess and determine your group's specific needs and then for you to choose skill building activities from the multiple list that best meets the needs of your group. The first activity in this section Working Towards Success is a needs assessment activity that collects feedback from the student, teacher, and parent. Once the specific needs of your group are determined then you can use the Correlation Chart on page 183 to select session activities. The Small Group Roster and Planning Form on page 19-20 can be helpful in writing down the group plans. For each session a main skill building activity needs to be selected as well as an icebreaker/energizer chosen (See Icebreakers/Energizers Section). An additional, optional component can be added to each group session – Service Learning (See the Service Learning Section for more information).

This book is designed in hopes of helping counselors to be focused on students' needs and to be efficient and effective in helping students.

School Success Skills

• INITIAL GROUP SESSION...

Review the Getting Started: First Group Session on page 17. Complete the Needs Assessment Activity C which includes a student and a parent/teacher needs assessment. Review the area of needs from these assessments and with the use of the Needs Assessment Correlation to School Success Skill Building Activities Chart on page 183, plan the skill building activities for the remaining group sessions.

• SKILL BUILDING ACTIVITIES ...

The following is a list of School Success Skills building activities grouped by sub topics that relate to the needs assessment. Each activity will take about 20-25 minutes therefore only one activity needs to be planned for each group meeting. Not all activities will be used, only those that relate to the needs of your group. Select your activities, guided by your Needs Assessment Correlation to School Success Skill Building Activities Chart on page 183. You may also want to use the Small Group Roster and Planning Chart on pages 19-20 to organize your sessions and activities.

Listening and Attending Skills

Organizing

Study Tips

Homework Tips

Test Taking Tips

Attitude

• CLOSING GROUP SESSION...

Review the How to End: Final Group Session on page 23. Complete the Closing Activity C7 which includes a student and a parent/teacher post assessment. Use this information to evaluate the group and to determine follow up with individual students on continuing weaknesses.

NEEDS ASSESSMENT ACTIVITY C
Working Towards Success

Purpose: To assess the students' need for skill building for school success.

Materials Needed:
- Book Bag with the following information written on poster board strips and placed in the empty bag:
  - I behave well in class.
  - I stay focused and listen carefully in class.
  - I am organized.
  - I know how to study and learn material.
  - I complete my homework efficiently.
  - I know how to take tests and I do well.
  - I have a good attitude about school.
- Copy of the Student Needs Assessment for School Success Skills for each student
- Pencils

Procedures:
1. **Introduction:** Begin by playing the "why" game ... Ask: *Why is school important?* They may answer, "To learn." Ask: *Why do you want to learn?* Answer, "To get a good job." Ask: *Why do you want to get a good job?* Answer, "So you can have money for food, clothing, etc." End this exchange summarizing that school seems to be important in getting a good job for your future. Have students share what jobs/careers they may be interested in for their future.

2. Introduce that you have a story about Todd who has a job that he is not doing very well with. Encourage the students to listen to the story and try to figure out what job Todd has. Read Todd's story given below.

Todd has a job that he reports to Monday through Friday. He works a seven hour day. Part of Todd's job he does independently and part is supervised by his boss. Basically he just has to do what his boss tells him to do. But Todd is having problems. First, he is supposed to be at work at 8:00 but he usually arrives sometime around 8:20. By that time, his boss has already given out the duties for the day so he has to take time to go over Todd's with him again. Second, he usually arrives without his tools that he needs to do his job. He tries to borrow from his co-workers but they sometimes don't have extras to lend him. Also, Todd is not being effective in his job. Many times while he's supposed to be working, he starts thinking about what he would rather be doing. Todd has a difficult time doing what his boss says to do. Sometimes this is because Todd wasn't listening when his boss told him what to do and sometimes it's because Todd thinks he has a better way of doing the job. Most of the time, he ends up having to do things over again. Sometimes Todd will talk mean to his boss or his co-workers when he gets upset about having to do things over. Todd really doesn't seem to care, but his boss and his co-workers are getting tired of his ways.*

---

continued

After the story, have them point out the areas Todd is not doing well with such as: late for work, no supplies, not focusing, not following directions of his boss, being disrespectful to his boss and co-workers. Ask the students to guess what job he may have. Listen to their responses and then share with the students that Todd's job is that of a fourth grade student (or substitute the grade of the students in the group). Review the story again as the students relate the story to the job of a student in school. Emphasize that future success starts now in school.

3. Set the book bag in the center of group and explain that this is the book bag of a successful student. Tell them that we are going to take a look inside to find out the skills needed to be successful. Explain that as we review the skill cards from the bag it will also give us a chance to rate ourselves on where we are with these skills. Hand out the Needs Assessment sheet for School Success and explain that as each skill card is pulled from the bag they need to find that number on their sheet and rate themselves honestly. They need to mark a 4 if they strongly agree they have that skill, mark 3 if they agree they have that skill, mark 2 if they disagree about themselves having that skill and mark 1 if they strongly disagree. When all cards have been pulled from the book bag, ask them to complete questions 8 and 9 on their Needs Assessment sheet. Collect the sheets and share that this information from this sheet will be used to help plan what will be talked about in future small group sessions.

4. **Closure:** Encourage the students to think about and be aware of the things they do that helps them do well in school.

Explain to the students that you have a similar assessment for their parent and/or teacher to complete. Send copies with the students to give to their parent/teacher to complete and return. Or you may choose to put the Needs Assessment in teachers' boxes and mail to parents.

*reprinted with permission from 'Keys to Success' lesson in Puzzle Pieces: The Classroom Guidance Connection by Sitsch and Senn, Youthlight, 2002.

STUDENT NEEDS ASSESSMENT
For School Success

Name: _____

Directions: Complete the needs assessment as directed in the Working Towards Success Activity. Mark your answers honestly.

	STRONGLY AGREE	AGREE	DISAGREE	STRONGLY DISAGREE
1. I behave well in class.	4	3	2	1
2. I stay focused and listen carefully in class	4	3	2	1
3. I am organized.	4	3	2	1
4. I know how to study and learn material.	4	3	2	1
5. I complete my homework efficiently.	4	3	2	1
6. I know how to take tests.	4	3	2	1
7. I have a good attitude about school.	4	3	2	1

8. How would your teacher describe you as a student? _____

_____

9. How would you like your teacher to describe you as a student? _____

_____

PARENT/TEACHER NOTE
Needs Assessment

Dear Parent/Teacher,

Being successful in school is the foundation to a student's future. Utilizing the skills of listening, focusing, being organized, using time efficiently, knowing how to study, completing homework, knowing how to take tests and maintaining a good attitude are all essential skills in school success. These skills may come naturally to some children but for most of us these skills need to be taught, practiced, encouraged, structured, and maintained in order to be successful.

In our School Success Skills group we will be reviewing and strengthening these skills. However, we would appreciate your input regarding your child's present skills so that we can structure our group sessions on the group's needs. Review your child's present skills and complete the needs assessment given below and return. Please feel free to add comments or to share any information that would be helpful as we begin our small group. Thank you for your input as we work together to help our students be successful in school.

Sincerely,

Your Child's Counselor

PARENT/TEACHER NEEDS ASSESSMENT FOR

STUDENT/CHILD'S NAME _____

	STRONGLY AGREE	AGREE	DISAGREE	STRONGLY DISAGREE
1. He/she behaves well in class.	4	3	2	1
2. He/she stays focused and listens carefully in class	4	3	2	1
3. He/she is organized.	4	3	2	1
4. He/she knows how to study and learn material.	4	3	2	1
5. He/she completes his/her homework efficiently.	4	3	2	1
6. He/she knows how to take tests.	4	3	2	1
7. He/she has a good attitude about school.	4	3	2	1

Comments:

NEEDS ASSESSMENT CORRELATION

to Skill Building Activities for School Success Skills

Directions: Use the chart to assist in planning skill building activities for group sessions. Below is a listing of the activities as they relate to each statement in the needs assessments. Select an appropriate skill building activity for each session depending on the needs determined from the assessments as well as group discussions and observations. Area of needs may be indicated by a score of "1" or "2" on an item on the assessment. For an area of heavy need you may choose to plan for several sessions utilizing several skill building activities focusing on that sub topic. For lighter needs you may choose only one session choosing only one skill building activity from that sub topic. If there is no need indicated for that sub topic then do not plan to use a skill building activity from that area. Remember these skill building activities are written covering a wide range of information so that you may choose only the ones that fit the group's needs. All activities will not be used in a typical 6-8 session group.

NEEDS ASSESSMENT STATEMENTS

NEEDS ASSESSMENT STATEMENTS	SKILL BUILDING ACTIVITIES THAT CORRELATE		
1. I behave well in class.	C1.2	C1.3	
2. I stay focused and listen carefully in class	C1.1		
3. I am organized.	C2.1	C2.2	C2.3
4. I know how to study and learn material.	C3.1	C3.2	C3.3
5. I complete my homework efficiently.	C4.1	C4.2	
6. I know how to take tests.	C5.1	C5.2	C5.3
7. I have a good attitude about school.	C6.1	C6.2	

ACTIVITY C1.1
Focusing Power

Purpose: To share strategies to improve focusing and listening in class.

Materials Needed:
- The following items or a picture of the item placed in a bag:
  - Open eyes: open eyes taped on a pair of sunglasses or a picture of looking eyes
  - Radio head phone set
  - Picture of a raised hand
  - Picture of someone sitting up to a desk with good posture.
  - Pencil taped to a notepad
  - Write the words or draw a picture of "a sound proof bubble"
  - Question mark
- Chart paper and marker

Procedures:
1. **Introduction:** Ask if students have ever had their minds start to wander in class and later they realized they missed out on what the teacher was saying. Allow students to share.

2. Explain to the students that you have a bag full of things to help us listen well, to attend and stay focused on what we are supposed to be listening to. Share that the only problem is that you lost the directions to explain how each thing works in helping you be a good listener. Ask students if they think they could be of help. Take turns having students pull an item from the bag and asking the help of the group members to decide how the item would help improve listening and attending skills. Add the information below if it is not shared by the group. Write the new directions up on chart paper so you will have it for future use.

   - *Eyes:* Need to be looking at the person who is talking – listen and be tuned in. When the eyes wander our brain wanders.
   - *Radio head phone set:* It only has one channel – the teacher channel. Encourage students to stay tuned into the teacher while he/she is teaching and not be distracted by perhaps a neighbor whispering or someone walking down the hall.
   - *Raised hand:* Raise your hand to share an answer and be a part of the class discussion. It helps to stay tuned into the lesson when we are participating.
   - *Pencil and paper:* Take notes while listening to stay involved.
   - *Picture of Good Posture:* Sit up straight and tall so we can take in full breaths, get plenty of oxygen to the brain, and keep us awake to listen well.
   - *Sound proof bubble:* Use the bubble to pretend to close over you to block out other noise. However, the bubble has an intercom in it connected to the teacher.
   - *Question mark:* If you don't understand something – ask questions. So the teacher will not confuse you with a student that was daydreaming and not listening, don't just say, "I don't understand." Instead say, "I understand what you said about...but I'm having trouble with ..." or "I know how to do this part.... But I got lost when you said..."

   Summarize and review the new directions that have been written for good listening.

continued

3. To practice these listening skills play the game "Last Three Words." Instruct the students to listen well to you as you are talking, but when you stop they need to be able to tell you the last three words that were said. Before you begin with this exercise, encourage the students to sit up with eyes looking forward using their sound proof bubble or head phone set so they can do their best listening. You may choose a specific topic to talk about or begin reading a book, don't forget to stop in mid- sentence. After you stop, check what they think the last three words are. Either have them whisper them back to you or have them share with a partner or in group. Discuss if listening in this exercise is different than listening to TV or in a casual conversation. Point out that it takes energy to stay focused and be a good listener but it's this kind of listening that is important to learning in class.

4. **Closure:** Encourage the students to use these new strategies to help them listen well in class.

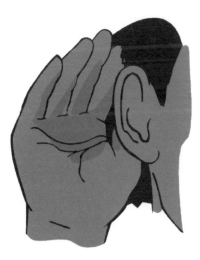

ACTIVITY C 1.2
Dealing with Distractions

Purpose: To share strategies for handling distractions.

Materials Needed:
- Set of magnets
- Storybook of any kind that group members can read and enjoy
- Chart paper and marker

Procedures:
1. **Introduction**: Ask students if they have ever been drawn into misbehaving in class or laughing at someone in class and got in trouble. Ask: *When we get side tracked in class does that interfere with listening to the teacher?* Ask them to share some things they have found that help them handle these distractions in an appropriate way so they can get back to listening and learning.

2. Display a set of magnets for the group. Demonstrate the attracting and repelling of magnets. Relate how we too are like these magnets - that at times it seems like we are drawn into the laughing or misbehaving. Therefore we need to either flip to the other side so we are not drawn to the distraction, or we can pretend to press the "de-magnetizing button" and not be drawn into the problem. Explain the de-magnetizing button giving the example of some store securities that have magnets in their tags. These tags on the item you are buying have to be cleared through their system or de-magnetized at check out so it does not set the alarm off as you leave the store.

3. Discuss ways to demagnetize or turn away so you can continue being a good listener. Write these suggestions on chart paper. You may want to add some strategies shared in Step 1. Include such ideas as:
   - keep your eyes looking at the teacher and focus on what is being said
   - turn your body away from the problem
   - pretend to press the de-magnetizing button as you use other strategies
   - remind yourself of the trouble you could get in if you join in on the misbehaving
   - remind yourself of the importance of listening to learn – remain focused on your goals for learning.

4. After summarizing and reviewing the strategies, have the students practice what they have learned. Ask a student to volunteer to read a story to the group (choose a simple storybook from your room or library) while the group practices their good listening skills. Warn them they need to continue listening even if there are distractions – encourage them to use their de-magnetizing button if necessary. While this story is being read to the group try to distract them with such behaviors as: thumping your pencil, humming, opening and closing the door, whispering at someone to get their attention, etc. Stop periodically and process with the group. Compliment those that maintained and challenge the others to try again. Rotate the reading of the story to several group members so all students have several opportunities to role play the de-magnetizing skill.

5. **Closure:** Challenge students to use this skill in the classroom when they need to avoid a problem and maintain good listening.

ACTIVITY C 1.3
Cooling It!

Purpose: To provide strategies for maintaining appropriate class behavior.

Materials Needed:
- Copy of the Cooling It! Activity sheet
- Plastic ice cubes (purchased from department stores) with the messages from the Ice Cube Activity sheet taped to each ice cube. Place these in the freezer to allow them to get cold before group.
- Blank ice cube messages from the Ice Cube Activity sheet for each student
- (Optional) A plastic ice cube for each student to take home

Procedures:
1. **Introduction:** Ask students to share their class rules. Discuss the reasons behind these rules. Conclude that the purpose of rules is to provide guidelines and structure so that learning can take place.

2. Share with the group that you want to tell them about the students in a class a few years ago. The students are good people but they did not follow the rules and their behavior interfered with their listening and learning. Share the pictures of each student from the Cooling It! Activity Sheet and describe their behavior. After each picture, ask the group to explain how the student's behavior interfered with their listening and learning. After all pictures have been shown, ask them to think about their behavior and see if there are any similarities between their behavior and the behavior of any in the pictures shared. They are welcome to share about themselves but not obligated.

3. Share that sometimes our behavior and talking can interfere with listening. Therefore we need to "cool it" with our behavior. Pull out the ice cubes with messages on each. Toss the ice cubes to the students and allow time for them to read the messages to the group and discuss how this might help. Add additional chill out messages the group may suggest.

4. Give each student a blank paper ice cube message. Have them write a "cool it" message that would help them the most in class. If you have extra plastic ice cubes to share, let them tape their message to an ice cube to take with them. If not, allow them to take their paper ice cube.

5. **Closure:** Encourage students to check their behavior in class to see if they are following the rules. If they are not following the rules, ask them to come up with a plan for improvement.

Cooling It! Activity Sheet

Directions: Copy, cut out, and fold along the dotted lines for use in procedure step 2.

Terry the Talker

Terry loves to talk and does so without thinking where he is or what's going on. A thought will "pop" into his head and he turns to a friend to share. Or in the middle of class he remembers that a friend left something at his house and he whispers across the rows to tell him when the teacher is in the middle of a lesson. Terry always has something to talk about to others. Do you think his behavior is a problem for listening and learning in class? Explain. (Add: Knowing how to talk is a good skill to have but you need to know when and where to talk.)

Class Clown Claude

Claude enjoys attention from others. He is always telling jokes and doing funny things to get people to look at him. He even makes funny noises in class when the teacher is teaching. I think he would even trip over his own feet if someone would laugh at him. Do you think his behavior is a problem for listening and learning in class? Explain. (Add: being a fun person to be around and helping others laugh is a good skill to have but it's important to know when and where to act silly.)

Cooling It! Activity Sheet

Directions: Copy, cut out, and fold along the dotted lines for use in procedure step 2.

Blurting Out Bill

Bill doesn't use his self control. The teacher can be in the middle of a sentence and Bill just interrupts with his question. Or in class he doesn't raise his hand he just yells out the answer or his comments. You can tell that Bill is always thinking because he's involved and sharing, but his interrupting sometimes keeps him and the class from understanding what the teacher is trying to say. Do you think his behavior is a problem for listening and learning in class? Explain. (Add: It's great that Bill is always thinking and he is actually very creative but it's important to learn and use self control to know when and where to share.)

Social Sally

Sally seems to know everyone and everything going on. She's always catching up on the 'lastest' from others. Sally is a great friend to be with at a party because she knows everyone. However Sally doesn't seem to care much about learning – she's too busy socializing. When the teacher calls on her she rarely knows where we are. Her mind always seems to be on the latest social event like the school dance, the student council election, or the upcoming spend the night party she's invited to. Do you think her behavior is a problem for listening and learning in class? Explain. (Add: It's great that Sally knows how to socialize but it's also important that she get a good educational foundation.)

Ice Cube Activity Sheet*

Directions: Copy, cut out, and tape these messages on to plastic ice cubes. Provide blank ice cube messages for each student.

Ice Cube Messages to "Cool" those behaviors that interfere with listening and learning.

Remind yourself of the consequences if you misbehave.

Keep your mouth closed if talking is getting you in trouble.

Ask your friends to help you by not trying to talk to you during the class time.

Ask your friends to help you by encouraging and reminding.

Remind yourself about the class rules.

Turn your brain on before talking.

Tell yourself not to talk now but to talk at recess or other OK times.

* Adapted with permission from Sitsch and Senn (2002). Puzzle Pieces Classroom Guidance Connection. Chapin, SC: YouthLight, Inc.

ACTIVITY C 2.1
I'll Find It!

Purpose: To assess the students' organizational skills and target areas and a plan for improvement.

Materials Needed:
- Variety of objects – different shapes and different color blocks, maybe different color miniature cars/trucks, etc.
- Copy of the Organization Quiz for each student.

Procedures:
1. **Introduction:** Dump a variety of objects on the table and have group members organize them in some way. Mix them up again and ask if another student has a different way the objects could be organized. Continue asking for different ways until all possibilities have been exhausted. (They may choose to organize them by shapes, colors, size, etc.) Point out the different feelings/thoughts when you look at the jumbled items vs. the items organized in some way. Most people have a calmer, ready to deal with it feeling/thought when things are organized. Discuss the hows of organization and the importance of organization for school success.

2. Ask students how organized they think they are. Tell them you have an Organization Quiz for them to find out how organized they really are. Hand out the quiz, read the directions and the statements as they mark. Ask them to score their sheet and answer the questions at the bottom. Let them share with the group their organizational strengths and weaknesses.

3. **Closure:** Encourage students to build on their organizational strengths and to implement a plan to improve their organizational weaknesses.

Organization Quiz

How organized are you? Take the quiz to find the answer. Mark 4 if you strongly agree, mark 3 if you agree, mark 2 if you disagree and mark 1 if you strongly disagree. Add up your points and see how you scored.

	STRONGLY AGREE	AGREE	DISAGREE	STRONGLY DISAGREE
1. My book bag is clean without trash and other "junk."	4	3	2	1
2. My school notebooks are organized by subject area and I have a folder or system for carrying papers home.	4	3	2	1
3. My school desk is neat and orderly.	4	3	2	1
4. I have an organized homework area at home with homework supplies.	4	3	2	1
5. I bring my school supplies to class.	4	3	2	1
6. I have a sheet, pad, or notebook for writing down homework assignments.	4	3	2	1
7. I bring the appropriate books and materials home to complete my homework assignments.	4	3	2	1
8. I remember to take my completed homework to school.	4	3	2	1
9. I make a plan ahead of time of how to complete long range assignments so I am not rushing at the last minute.	4	3	2	1
TOTAL				

Grand Total: _____

Add up your points and see how you scored:
- 34+   Great! Keep up the good work.
- 27-33   You're on the right track – keep working!
- 19-26   Looks like there is room for improvement.
- 9-18   Uh-Oh!

Review your answers:

What are your top two strongest areas of organization? _____

What are your two weakest areas that need improvement? _____

What is your plan for improvement? _____

_____

ACTIVITY 2.2
Super Scheduler to the Rescue!

Purpose: To assist students in their organizational skills by promoting the use of assignment sheets and schedulers.

Materials Needed:
- Copy of the Homework Assignment sheet for each student
- Copy of the Super Scheduler for each student

Procedures:

1. **Introduction:** Ask: *Have you ever gotten home from school and you sit down to do your homework and then you can't remember the page for the assignment? Or you get to school the next day and the teacher calls for an assignment and you don't have it either because you forgot you had to do it or you ran out of time to do your homework? How does it feel when you haven't quite got it together.* Explore with the students as to why we may not always be prepared. Suggest ideas like don't know how, don't want to take the time, too busy with other things, forgetful, work is too hard, etc. Tell the students that sometimes it is worth a bit of extra energy and effort in order to get it together so you can feel good about what you are doing. Let the students know that you have some forms and tips to help with the organization.

2. Give to each student a copy of the Homework Assignment sheet. (If your school already uses a different type of assignment sheet or perhaps an agenda notebook, replace this sheet with what your school requires for assignments). Review the assignment sheet having the students explain how to use it. Encourage students to always write down their assignments. If you are a list maker yourself – show and tell how you need to make lists in your job to stay focused on the important things that need to be accomplished each day.

3. Ask: *Has the TV monster ever grabbed you? Have ever sat down to watch just one 30 minute show but then the advertisements for the next show came on … and it also looked good so you sat for one more… but then the ad for the next show came on… and it looked good so you sat for one more show…, etc. until your parent called that it was time for bed and you realized you hadn't done your homework yet? Say: To the rescue to fight the TV and other time gobbling monsters is the Super Schedule Manager!* Give each student a copy of the Super Schedule Manager and allow time for each student to complete the correct month and dates on the calendar. Talk about the super powers of this scheduler to organize the afternoons in order to use the time to the fullest making sure to schedule in a time for homework. Show how due dates of long range assignments can be added in the space by the monthly dates. Have students brainstorm other information and activities that could by added to their calendar. You may include such activities as: baseball practice, scout meeting, playing outside, watching TV, practicing piano, etc. Include the idea of the importance to confer with their parents in setting up their calendar for the month so they can be aware of family events and schedules. Allow time for them to complete as much on their schedule as they can. Ask them to follow up with their parents to review their schedule and help them add information.

continued

4. **Closure:** Encourage students to use their homework assignments sheet to write down their assignments and to complete and use their super scheduler. Ask them to make sure there is a time for homework each week day on their schedule and that they follow their schedule. Completing homework and studying is one of the basics to school success.

WEEKLY HOMEWORK ASSIGNMENTS

NAME_____ DATE_____

Place a check mark in the boxes below when your assignment is complete.

SUBJECT	MONDAY	THUESDAY	WEDNESDAY	THURSDAY	FRIDAY
	☐	☐	☐	☐	☐
	☐	☐	☐	☐	☐
	☐	☐	☐	☐	☐
	☐	☐	☐	☐	☐
	☐	☐	☐	☐	☐
THINGS TO TAKE HOME					
THINGS TO BRING TO SCHOOL					
MESSAGES					

MONTH:

SUNDAY	MONDAY	TUESDAY	WEDNESDAY	THURSDAY	FRIDAY	SATURDAY
3:00 4:00 5:00 6:00 7:00 8:00	3:00 4:00 5:00 6:00 7:00 8:00	3:00 4:00 5:00 6:00 7:00 8:00	3:00 4:00 5:00 6:00 7:00 8:00	3:00 4:00 5:00 6:00 7:00 8:00	3:00 4:00 5:00 6:00 7:00 8:00	3:00 4:00 5:00 6:00 7:00 8:00
3:00 4:00 5:00 6:00 7:00 8:00	3:00 4:00 5:00 6:00 7:00 8:00	3:00 4:00 5:00 6:00 7:00 8:00	3:00 4:00 5:00 6:00 7:00 8:00	3:00 4:00 5:00 6:00 7:00 8:00	3:00 4:00 5:00 6:00 7:00 8:00	3:00 4:00 5:00 6:00 7:00 8:00
3:00 4:00 5:00 6:00 7:00 8:00	3:00 4:00 5:00 6:00 7:00 8:00	3:00 4:00 5:00 6:00 7:00 8:00	3:00 4:00 5:00 6:00 7:00 8:00	3:00 4:00 5:00 6:00 7:00 8:00	3:00 4:00 5:00 6:00 7:00 8:00	3:00 4:00 5:00 6:00 7:00 8:00
3:00 4:00 5:00 6:00 7:00 8:00	3:00 4:00 5:00 6:00 7:00 8:00	3:00 4:00 5:00 6:00 7:00 8:00	3:00 4:00 5:00 6:00 7:00 8:00	3:00 4:00 5:00 6:00 7:00 8:00	3:00 4:00 5:00 6:00 7:00 8:00	3:00 4:00 5:00 6:00 7:00 8:00
3:00 4:00 5:00 6:00 7:00 8:00	3:00 4:00 5:00 6:00 7:00 8:00	3:00 4:00 5:00 6:00 7:00 8:00	3:00 4:00 5:00 6:00 7:00 8:00	3:00 4:00 5:00 6:00 7:00 8:00	3:00 4:00 5:00 6:00 7:00 8:00	3:00 4:00 5:00 6:00 7:00 8:00

ACTIVITY 2.3
Planning Ladder*

Purpose: To assist students in their organization skills for long range projects and overwhelming tasks by learning the 'how to' and promoting the use of a planning form.

Materials Needed:
- Chart paper and marker
- Popsicle sticks, 7-8 for each student and yourself
- Copy of the Planning Ladder Sheet, two for each student and yourself
- Glue

Procedures:
1. **Introduction:** Draw a ladder on chart paper with four steps. Ask the students how most people get to the top of a ladder. Come to the conclusion that we start at the bottom and take one step at a time to reach the top. Point out to the group that it is not safe to skip steps, and you do not usually see a person go up two steps then down one then skip to the fourth then back to the first. Most people know how to go up a ladder from watching others successfully go up one step at a time until they reach the top. Ask them to think about how steps can be helpful in completing a long range assignment. Have students give examples of long range assignments they have had such as: book reports, learning their 12 multiplication tables by a certain date, or science projects due.

2. The first steps to being successful with a long range assignment is to first specify the steps or details needed to complete the project (on the bottom step of the ladder you drew on the chart paper, write: List Steps). Next prioritize the details as to what comes first, second, and third in your project (add to your next step up on your ladder the word: Prioritize). Then add a time frame for each detail or step to be completed (to your next step add: Time/Date for Step Completion). The final step is to do it!
(On your top step write: Do It!). Give to each student a copy of the Planning Ladder sheet. Explain to them that these steps can be used to plan long range assignments as well as used to organize overwhelming tasks like cleaning your room or completing a project.

3. Get the students' help to plan for a pretend science project that is due in 4 weeks. Have them brainstorm the steps for success needed (Steps may include: Research and select topic, list and locate materials needed, implement experiment, complete rough draft of written information and results of experiment, complete final paper/presentation). Write each step on a popsicle stick and then get the groups' help to prioritize the steps and put them in order adding a time for completion for each. Glue these completed popsicle sticks to the steps on the Planning Ladder sheet.

continued

4. Give each student 7-8 popsicle sticks. Assign each student one of the possible difficult or long range assignments given below. Instruct each student to review their assignment and then organize it according to the "Ladder Technique" of listing steps, prioritizing, etc. Have them complete the steps on their popsicle sticks, organize them and glue the sticks to their ladder on the Planning Ladder sheet. Allow the students to share their steps for project completion with the group.
    *   You have one hour to clean up your messy bedroom
    *   You have to know your 12 multiplication tables in 2 weeks
    *   You have a book report due in 4 weeks
    *   You have a research paper on the Civil War due in 3 weeks
    *   Your notebook and book bag are a mess and you can't find your homework.

5. **Closure:** Encourage students to use the Planning Ladder to help them be successful in dealing with long range assignments or overwhelming tasks.

Adapted with permission from Sitsch and Senn (2002). Puzzle Pieces… The Classroom Guidance Connection. Chapin, SC: YouthLight, Inc.

Long Range Planner Ladder

Assignement:_____

Date:_____

STEP SIX

Date/Time Completed

STEP FIVE

Date/Time Completed

STEP FOUR

Date/Time Completed

STEP THREE

Date/Time Completed

STEP TWO

Date/Time Completed

STEP ONE

Date/Time Completed

ACTIVITY 3.1
Memory Magic

Purpose: To assist students in using memory tips and strategies to remember information that is important to learn.

Materials Needed:
- Black top hat that magicians traditionally use. (Plastic black top hats can usually be found at a party goods store.)
- Copy and cut out the rabbits on Memory Magic Activity sheet. Place these inside the hat.
- Copy blank rabbits for each student

Procedures:
1. **Introduction:** Set the black top hat on the table with the top of the hat down and ask students what magicians usually pull out of hats. Search for the word "rabbit". Tell them that you don't think you can pull out a real rabbit from the hat but there is something magical about the rabbits that are going to be pulled from the hat. Explain that the rabbits will share about a different kind of magic called "memory magic". Ask the students what they think memory magic is all about. After hearing their answers summarize that memory magic is simply learning helpful tricks to remember information that is important to learn.

2. Direct a student to pull a rabbit out of the hat and see what he has to say. When they pull a rabbit out of the hat either you read or have the student read the memory magic information. Allow time to discuss, elaborating when and how that memory tip might be helpful. Give examples of each memory magic tip. Let each student take turns pulling a rabbit out and leading the discussion.

3. After all rabbits have been pulled from the hat and discussed, give each student a blank rabbit. Instruct them to think about memory tips that have been discussed and write on their rabbit the memory magic tips they think will be most helpful for them to use.

4. **Closure:** Let students know that the true magic is in them. For it is in themselves that they can use strategies and memory tips to help them be successful in learning.

Memory Magic Activity Sheet

Directions: Copy front and back and cut out the memory magic rabbits. Place the rabbits in a magician's top hat to be pulled out and discussed in group. Copy and cut out a blank rabbit for each student for them to add memory ideas of their own or to summarize a helpful tip.

What does it remind me of?
Create a funny thought or story in your head to help you remember.

Picture It!
Draw a picture of the fact to remember

Sing it!
Put the information in a song or rhyme to help remember.

Say it out loud.
Reading the information out loud can help you learn the information especially if you are an auditory learner.

Memory Magic Activity Sheet

Example:
For the Mayflower landing in American in 1620 - draw an outline of a ship with the year 1620 written on it.

Example:
Herbert Hoover was the 21st president of the United States. (Place the name Hoover on the floor with a Hoover vacuum cleaner with the racing number 21 on it vacuuming up the name.)

Example:
In 1492 Columbus sailed the ocean blue.

202

Memory Magic Activity Sheet

Draw it in the air
Pretend to be writing the notes or spelling words in the air.

Count the letters of the spelling word
Count the number of letters in your spelling words –sometimes the number can clear up letter confusion.

Create and use secret codes (Mnemonic devices)
For memorizing words in a series, take the first letter of each word and create a new word or name.

Create and use secret codes (Mnemonic devices)
Take the first letter in each word and create a silly sentence in which each word also begins with the same letter.

Memory Magic Activity Sheet

Example:
The spelling word "really" has 6 letters. The number six may help you remember that it has two "l's" instead of one.

Example:
Our nine planets in the solar system - from the closest to the farthest from the sun: Mercury, Venus, Earth, Mars, Jupiter, Saturn, Uranus, Neptune, and Pluto. - *"My very educated mother just served us nine pizzas."*

Example:
Colors of the rainbow: Red, Orange, Yellow, Green Blue, Indigo, Violet - *"Roy G. Biv"*

ACTIVITY C3.2
Information Recall

Purpose: To provide strategies to organize information so that it becomes easier to learn and remember.

Materials Needed:
- Prepare envelopes containing the information on the Information Recall Activity sheet
- Chart paper and marker
- Consult with their teacher(s) before the group meeting to gather information, materials, and key points that will be covered on an upcoming test. Select a subject that involves information recall such as Social Studies, Health, or Science in which outline, webbing and the use of notecards is helpful in preparing for the test.

Procedures:
1. **Introduction:** Say: *Your mission, if you choose to accept, is to learn the information for your upcoming (name a subject area – Social Studies, Health, Science) test. The strategies in the following envelopes may be of use. Digest the evidence after you read it.* Hand each pair of students an envelope with a strategy for organizing and learning information. Direct them to open their envelopes, read, and be prepared to share that information with the group.

2. Take turns having students share the information in their envelopes. As a strategy is discussed, use the specific information you gathered from the teacher before group and organize the information according to the strategy. Add this example to the chart paper. For instance, if the strategy is webbing, then as a group, organize the information for the test in web form. If you are unable to get specific information just talk in general as to how to utilize the informational organizational strategy.

3. **Closure:** Encourage students to take the time to organize information so that it becomes easier to learn and remember.

Information Recall Activity

Directions: Copy and cut apart the following information organization strategies and place in envelopes (one strategy per envelope). Have students read and share with the group the information.

Review your notes from class highlighting important words. If the information is grouped in sets then use different color highlighters. Add pictures or any other memory triggers to help retain the information. Read your notes silently, read your notes outloud (especially for auditory learners) and then reread them again.

NoteTaking

OUTLINE
(Topic)

I. Main Idea
  A. Sub Point
  B. _____
  C. _____
    1. Facts/ Details
    2. _____

II. 2nd Main Idea
  A. _____
  B. _____

Outline

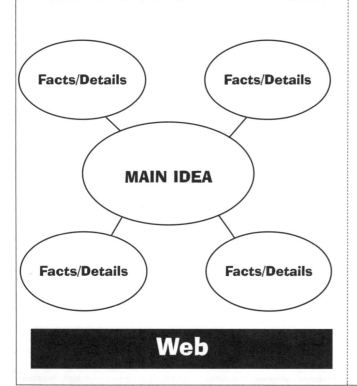

Facts/Details **Facts/Details**

MAIN IDEA

Facts/Details **Facts/Details**

Web

Put important notes in question/answer format on index type cards with the question on one side and the answer on the other. Place the cards in a stack and begin quizzing yourself. Place the cards you know in a "Do Know" pile and the ones you don't know or unsure of in a "Don't Know" pile. Then restudy the "Don't Know" pile until you know it all and are prepared for the test.

Flash Cards

ACTIVITY C3.3
Learner Types

Purpose: To identify the student's learning style strength and to utilize this information to enhance learning.

Materials Needed:
- Picture cards from the Learner Types Activity sheet copied and cut apart. (Need about six of each picture card per student)
- Chart paper and marker
- Pencils

Procedures:

1. **Introduction:** Ask: *Who in the group thinks they learn best from listening to the words of the teacher? How many learn best from looking at pictures, drawings, or graphs? How many learn best by doing things?* Share with them that different people learn best in different ways and that it's important to know where your strengths are in order to focus on learning in that way.

2. Explain that the three top ways in which people learn are visually, auditorially, and hands-on (kinesthetically). The visual learner learns best by watching or observing – with their eyes. The auditory learner learns best by listening – with their ears. The hands-on learner learns best by doing and being involved – with their hands/body. Share that you have an activity to help them find out where they are strongest in learning. Place the three stacks of learning style cards in the center (stack of ear cards, eye cards and hand cards). Explain that you will ask a series of multiple choice questions and they will be directed to answer their question by selecting either an Eye Card, an Ear Card, or a Hand Card. They are to place the card they selected in front of them. Cards will be tallied at the end of the activity. Ask the following questions.

   a. *When you are in class, do you learn the new information better when the teacher:*
      lectures - if so select an ear card
      shows or demonstrates the information - if so select an eye card
      or creates a game or activity – if so select a hand card.
   b. *When you read information in a textbook do you learn the information better by:*
      reading the information out loud – if so select an ear card
      reading the information silently – if so select an eye card
      or singing and tapping on your book while you read – if so select a hand card.
   c. *If you could choose how to present a book report, would you rather:*
      give an oral report, telling about your book – if so select an ear card
      write a report – if so select an eye card
      act out the story or create a model of the book – if so select a hand card.
   d. *When you are listening to the teacher teach, what do you do to stay focused? Do you:*
      follow along in the book – if so select an eye card
      raise your hand to get involved in the discussion – if so select an ear card
      or take notes – if so select a hand card.

continued

e. *When you are memorizing lines for a play do you learn best by:*
   saying the lines over and over out loud – if so select an ear card
   reading and studying the lines silently – if so select an eye card.

f. *When you are improving in a sport would you rather*
   listen to the coach explain how to improve – if so select an ear card
   observe others playing the sport well – if so select an eye card
   or playing the sport – if so select a hand care

g. *Do you feel you can best tell what you know when you can:*
   show or display something – if so select an eye card
   discuss it with someone – if so select an ear card
   write or draw about it – if so select a hand card

h. *When playing a new game, do you understand the rules better if you:*
   read them silently to yourself – if so select an eye card
   listen while someone reads them aloud to you – if so select the ear card
   or start playing and just learn as you go along – if so select the hand card.

Direct each student to add up the number of eye, ear and hand cards they selected. If they have more eye cards then they probably learn best by observing and are visual learners, if they have more ear cards then they learn best by listening and are auditory learners, and if they have more hand cards then they learn best by doing and they are hands-on or kinesthetic learners.

3. Divide the chart paper by drawing lines into thirds and taping a different learning style card (the eye, ear, and hand card) to each section. Discuss with the students how a person who is strong in that particular learning style might choose to listen in class, complete homework, and study for a test so they can be learning at their best. Add this information to the chart paper. Include the following in the discussion.

   • For the **Visual Learner** (eye card): Sit near the front of the class where you can see the board, etc. Take class notes. Add pictures and charts to class notes to help remember the information. In studying for a test reread the notes, study guides or textbook pages several times. Create flash cards to help you study.

   • For the **Auditory Learner** (ear card): Sit in the class where you can hear well and focus on what the teacher is saying. Read your textbook pages, study guide or notes outloud several times. Create a song or rhyme to help remember facts. Record important information on a tape recorder and play it back.

   • For the **Hands-On or Kinesthetic Learner** (hand card): Use puppets or other characters to retell the important facts in studying information. Draw pictures, sing, or act out information to learn. Pretend to write the spelling words in the air. Practice multiplication facts by writing them with sidewalk chalk, with finger paints, or better yet in the sand at the beach!

4. **Closure:** Ask each student to take a learning style card (eye, ear, or hand) that is their strength, turn it over, and write down some helpful hints from their area listed on the chart paper that may be of help. Encourage the students to add these strategies to their learning routine.

Learning Style Activity Sheet

Directions: Copy and cut apart the learning style cards. Need at least six cards of each picture for each student. Stack all of the eye cards together, the ear cards together, and the hand cards together and place the stacks in the center of the group. Leader needs to read the multiple choice questions given in procedure step 2 of the activity allowing students to select a card according to their answer. At the end of the activity, tally the cards to indicate the learning strength of the student.

Visual Learner

Visual Learner

Hands-on Learner

Hands-on Learner

Auditory Learner

Auditory Learner

Learning Style Activity Sheet

ACTIVITY C 4.1
Homework Time!

Purpose: To provide information on good homework habits.

Materials Needed:
- Picture sets from the Homework Time! Activity Sheet
- Empty shoe box for each student
- Construction paper, scissors, glue, tape
- Chart paper and marker

Procedures:

1. **Introduction:** Ask: *Have you heard this saying, 'a picture is worth a thousand words'? What does it mean?* Conclude that pictures carry messages. Share with the students that you have three sets of pictures with messages entitled "What's Wrong With This Picture?" and "What's Right With This Picture?" Share the sets of pictures from the Homework Time! Activity Sheet and follow the procedure steps 2, 3 and 4 to guide the discussion.

2. Discussion of Set One Pictures: Say: *I'm sure that it has never happened to you before but perhaps you have known someone who has gotten home from school, sat down to do their homework and realized that they left a book they needed at school!* Point out the importance of taking time to pack up the correct materials. Focus on the "Stop Sign" in the second picture. Explain to the students how to use the stop sign to help them pack up at the end of the day: STOP – Last 5 minutes of the day "stop"; THINK – Think about books and materials needed for homework; GO – pack up all needed materials.

3. Discussion of Set Two Pictures: Point out how difficult it is to concentrate and complete the homework with distractions such as the TV, phone, toys, etc. Emphasize the importance of setting up a private, quiet study area whether it be at a desk or a place at the kitchen table. Study at the same place each day and try to study at the same time to establish the routine. Ask students to tell about their study area. Elaborate on additional study tips such as:

   - Study your hardest subject first (you have more energy when you first sit down to study therefore you can tackle the difficult subject and complete it in less time than if you wait until the end of the study time when you are more tired.)
   - Take short stretch breaks between subjects.
   - If you have difficulty staying focused on your work, use a timer and challenge yourself to complete the assignment in a set amount of time.
   - If you have a tendency to rush through your homework set a mandatory study time allotment for homework, typically 10 minutes per grade level (for example: 40 minutes of study time for a 4th grader). If homework is finished ahead of time, still use that time to study ahead, read, or review spelling words for the test at the end of the week.

continued

- When homework is completed, place it in your bookbag and set your bookbag and any other materials you need to take to school in your "Drop Spot". A "Drop Spot" is a designated area somewhere in your room or by the exit door where your bookbag and other materials are placed ready to be picked up on the way out the door heading to school in the mornings.

  (If time permits allow the students to also make "Do Not Disturb" and "Drop Spot" signs.)

4. Discussion of Set Three Pictures: Stress the importance of having the materials you need to complete homework so that you do not lose time searching through your place looking for a pencil or glue or what ever you need to complete the homework. Point out the homework kit in the second picture. Have the students brainstorm together the kinds of things they typically need for their homework that would be important to put in the kit. List these items on chart paper. Hand each student a shoe box, construction paper, staples, scissors, tape, etc. Allow each student to create/decorate their own homework kit box to take home, to add important homework supplies and to place in their homework area ready to use. (If you have extra supplies and you feel there is a need, you may choose to hand out some basic supplies for their box).

5. **Closure:** Encourage students to evaluate their present homework habits and procedures and make changes if needed.

Homework Time! Activity Sheet

Directions: Discuss each set of pictures and decide "what's wrong" and "what's right" with each set.

What's Wrong With This Picture?	What's Right With This Picture?

What's Wrong With This Picture?	What's Right With This Picture?

What's Wrong With This Picture?	What's Right With This Picture?

ACTIVITY C4.2
Homework Frustrations

Purpose: To provide problem solving solutions for managing homework frustrations.

Materials Needed:
- Cards from the Homework Frustrations Activity sheet copied and cut apart
- pencils

Procedures:

1. **Introduction:** Ask: *Have you ever gotten frustrated with your homework before?* Encourage students to share connecting their stories to others with similar experiences. Add that when homework is frustrating the thought may cross our minds that it is easier to give up and quit – easier but not the best way to handle it. Ask students to share appropriate ways they have found that have helped them handle their homework frustrations. As they share, compliment them on searching for and finding ways to manage the frustrations.

2. Ask for their help as good problem solvers. Hand to each student a frustrating homework situation written on a card from the Homework Frustrations Activity sheet. Instruct them to read the information adding their own thoughts and/or answering the question. Ask them to be prepared to share and teach their information to the group. You may choose to let the students work on these in pairs or individually. If additional homework frustrations other than those listed on the activity sheet were shared in procedure #1 then you may want to add a card with that frustration for students to problem solve. Allow time for students to share and teach the information on their card. Open the discussion to the group adding additional information. If you have access to a school newsletter, consider letting your group sponsor a "Homework Problem Solvers" column to include these ideas they worked on in group. Make sure they get to add their names to the article.

3. **Closure:** Encourage students to put into practice when needed their great ideas!

Homework Frustrations Activity Sheet

Directions: Copy and cut apart the homework frustrations/problem solving cards. Have students work to add additional problem solving information and then share/teach it to the group.

1. When you don't understand how to do the homework assignment …

   - re-read the directions
   - look for and study the examples that may be given
   - take a 10 minute break to clear your mind and try again
   - call a classmate
   - ask a parent only after you have tried to figure it out
   - if you are still unable to understand the assignment, write a note to the teacher explaining what you're are having trouble with and asking for help.

   Other Thoughts:

   _____
   _____
   _____
   _____
   _____
   _____
   _____

2. When you're feeling overwhelmed like you'll never finish the assignment then…

   - Divide the assignment into smaller parts and take one step at a time.
   - Cover the problems with a sheet of paper that you are not working on and take one problem at a time.
   - Set time limits/challenges to prompt focusing on completing a problem – then take a stretch break – then begin the next problem.

   Other Thoughts:

   _____
   _____
   _____
   _____
   _____
   _____
   _____
   _____
   _____

Homework Frustrations Activity Sheet

3. When you don't have the confidence that you can do the homework and you don't want to try anymore, then give yourself an encouraging talk such as…

_____
_____
_____
_____
_____
_____
_____
_____
_____
_____
_____
_____
_____
_____

4. When you feel that you are missing out on fun stuff because of homework then…

- minimize distractions and tell yourself "work before play"
- use a daily planner to schedule homework and fun things too
- compliment yourself for sticking with and completing the assignment – that's called perseverance!
- set up a personal reward system such as, "I will listen to music (play video games, etc) for 15 minutes after the homework is done."

Other Thoughts:

_____
_____
_____
_____
_____
_____
_____

5. When parents check your homework and it's not correct and you have to redo it – what could you think, say, or do to help with this frustration?

- Think about how it is important to learn and get it right even if it does take extra time.
- Think: this may help to get a better grade.
- Don't argue, just do it! (arguing only makes it longer and complicates the problem)

Other Thoughts:

_____
_____
_____
_____
_____
_____
_____
_____

6. When you question the importance of having to do homework, remember …

- Homework is a chance to practice what I'm learning.
- Homework = learning = future career = money= more time for fun

Other Thoughts:

_____
_____
_____
_____
_____
_____
_____
_____
_____

ACTIVITY C5.1
Gearing Up for the Test

Purpose: To review helpful tips in preparing for a test and to emphasize the importance of reading and following directions.

Materials Needed:
- For each student copy, and laminate talk bubble on the Gearing up for the Test Activity sheet.
- Copy of This is a Test sheet for each student.
- Pencils and erasable markers for each student
- Chart paper and marker

Procedures:
1. **Introduction:** Ask students how they feel about taking tests. Summarize the feelings shared and explore the why behind some of the feelings (perhaps a reason for a negative feeling about the test is they don't feel prepared or ready for the test). Ask students to share helpful tips they may have found to prepare and get ready to take a test. Information may include studying ahead for the test, finding out exactly what material the test covers, knowing what type of test will be given, etc.

2. Hand to each person a talk bubble from the Gearing Up for the Test Activity sheet and an erasable marker. Tell the students that knowing what material the test covers and the important points of the material is essential to doing well on a test. Point out that teachers give clues all along – we just have to tune in. Ask students to write on their talk bubble something a teacher might say to indicate that a particular piece of information is important to know and will probably be on the test. Allow time for the students to write and share with the group. You may choose for them to write and share again if they have other statements to share. Some things a teacher might say to indicate the material is important are:
   - Make sure you learn this!
   - Know this material!
   - Pay attention now!
   - Don't forget…
   - Listen!
   - Memorize…
   - You will find this on the test.
   - The main ideas in this unit are…
   - This is important!
   - Get this down on paper.

continued

3. Tell the students that after you have prepared for the test, next you have to know how to take the test. Let them know you have a quick test you want them to take today. Hand out the This is a Test sheet and pencils. Instruct them to read the directions first and begin. This is a test to stress the importance of reading and following directions. If they truly read the directions and follow them then they will not be doing/answering all of the silly questions. Allow students to complete the test and then ask them what they learned from the test. Ask if they have ever missed parts on a test and made a lower grade because they did not take the time to read and follow the directions. Once again stress the importance of following directions. Have students brainstorm key words and directions that can be tricky sometimes. Write these on chart paper. Include such key directions as:
   • write in complete sentences
   • check your spelling
   • use correct punctuation
   • underline the subject once and the predicate twice
   • reduce to lowest terms
Point out to students to also tune into key words such as: always, never, all, only, except, after, and before.

4. **Closure:** Encourage students to tune into the words of the teacher to know important material and to carefully read and follow directions on the test.

Gearing Up for the Test Activity Sheet

Directions: Copy and laminate the talk bubble for each student. Instruct students to write on their talk bubble things a teacher might say to indicate that the specific material is important to learn and may be on a test.

This Is A Test

Directions: Read all the questions on the page before beginning and follow the directions carefully.

1. Write your full name. _____

2. On the back of the page write the numbers from 1-25 backwards.

3. Look at the person sitting beside you and write down the color of their eyes. _____

4. If you could be a famous person who would you be?

    _____

5. Say your teacher's name out loud three times.

6. Stand beside your desk and do three jumping jacks.

7. Ignore all of the above directions. Sign your name at the bottom and be quiet so no one else catches on.

ACTIVITY C5.2
Test Types

Purpose: To explore strategies for successfully taking different types of tests.

Materials Needed:
- Information on test taking strategies such as Lee and Marlene Canter's *What To Do When Your Child Needs To Study* (pp. 40-44). Canter and Associates, Inc. 1-800-262-4347
- Copy of the Test Types Activity Sheet
- Dice

Procedures:
1. **Introduction:** Ask: *Have you ever felt like you knew the material yet you didn't do well on the test? Has the wording on the test or the test type ever confused you?*

2. Display the Test Types Activity sheet and review the different types listed. Ask students to share which type test they prefer and why. Say: *Since we have all those different types of tests at different times we need your help to share any tips you have on how to successfully take that type of test.* Take turns rolling the dice. Correlate the number on the dice to the test type and share one tip or strategy you can think of to help take that test. If the student can not think of a suggestion then they need to ask and call on someone else in the group who has a suggestion. (Be on stand-by to share good strategies. The information in the Canter's What To Do When Your Child Needs To Study may be a good resource.)

3. (Option) Instead of talking about the different types of test, you may choose to talk about how to prepare for different subject area tests such as: Spelling, Math, Social Studies, Reading and Science/Health. Simply list the subject areas on paper to display with the different dice numbers 1-6 included. Roll the dice and play the game as described in Step 2.

4. **Closure:** Encourage students to use these strategies to successfully take different types of tests.

Test Type Activity Sheet

Directions: Copy and display for the group. Take turns rolling the dice and sharing tips and strategies for successfully taking that type of test. If a six is rolled then they can choose any test type to talk about.

- ⚀ True/False Test
- ⚁ Multiple - Choice Test
- ⚂ Essay Test
- ⚃ Fill in the Blank Test
- ⚄ Open Book Test
- ⚅ Your Choice

ACTIVITY C5.3
Test Stress

Purpose: To provide strategies for dealing with test stress.

Materials Needed:
- Create a Stress Solutions Ball by writing the following statements on a ball with a permanent magic marker.
  - Take 2 deep breaths and clear your mind of worries!
  - Give yourself a pep talk to relax and do your best!
  - Shake your hands, roll your shoulders and tell yourself to relax and turn your brain on.
  - Clarify any confusing questions with the teacher if needed.
  - Remind yourself that you are prepared for the test because you studied ahead of time.
  - Maintain confidence in your ability. Repeat to yourself, "I can do it, I can do it, I can!"
- Provide balls for each student to design and keep
- Permanent markers for each student's use
- Chart paper and marker

Procedures:
1. **Introduction:** Ask: *Have you ever studied, prepared for a test, and knew the material and yet when it was time for the test you seemed to get uptight and stressed out to the point that you could not remember the information?* Allow time for students to share and connect to other people's experiences. Explain that the best way to help with this is to reduce the feelings of stress so the brain can work.

2. Show the prepared Stress Solutions Ball indicating strategies for reducing stress. Take turns tossing the ball to group members. As a student catches the ball, tell them to look where their index finger of their right hand is pointing and share that stress reduction tip with the group. Allow time for demonstration of the strategy and discussion. Continue tossing the ball until all information is shared.

3. Review the stress reduction strategies listed on the ball. Ask students for any additional ideas or suggestions. You may choose to summarize the strategies on chart paper and add additional ideas.

4. Give each student a plain stress ball and marker. Instruct the students to choose their top stress reduction strategies that they feel would be helpful to them and write it on their ball to take with them.

5. **Closure:** Encourage students to use the strategies and suggestions on their stress ball to alleviate the test stress so they can succeed in doing their best on the test.

ACTIVITY C6.1
Motivation

Purpose: To encourage the students to think positive, encouraging thoughts about the importance of school in order to stay motivated to do their best.

Materials Needed:
- Copy and cut out the think bubble on the Motivation Activity sheet for each student
- Paper and pencil

Procedures:
1. **Introduction:** Ask if anyone keeps up with the top ten list in songs or movies? Let them elaborate and ask them what it means to be in the top ten list and how that list might be chosen.

2. Tell them that you need their help to come up with a top five list. Tell them you need them to determine the top five reasons why school is important. Explain that this needs to be a group activity. Take suggestions as to how to go about the process to determine this. Possible procedures are: group members may write their thoughts on why school is important on a sheet of paper and then compile all the suggestions and vote to select and prioritize the top five list. Or they may choose to have a group leader to facilitate a discussion. If the group chooses this method, you may want to briefly define qualities of a leader as including all, listening to all suggestions, keeping the group focused on the task, summarizing the progress of the group and prompting or redirecting, etc. If leadership style is chosen, rotate the position of leader with the counselor being the recorder and taking notes. Guide students into choosing the group procedure and help them structure how they will go about following through with the task. After the initial help, allow the group to take the leadership. When the task is complete, review and share their top five list. Make sure to compliment the students on their work. If students are willing, share their results with administration and/or publish in the school newsletter.

3. Hand each student a think bubble from the Motivation Activity sheet and a pencil. Ask students to think about what they tell themselves or think to themselves to stay motivated about school. Instruct them to write this on their think bubble. Have the students take turns holding their thought bubble beside their head and sharing the information with the group.

4. **Closure:** Encourage students to continue using these thoughts to motivate them to stay focused on doing their best at school.

Motivation Activity Sheet

Directions: Copy a thought bubble for each student. Think about what to tell yourself or think about to stay motivated about school. Write this on the think bubble and share with the group.

ACTIVITY C6.2
Excuses... Excuses

Purpose: To help the student be aware of excuses we may make about school to delay or get out of needed work and to change these negative thoughts to positive thoughts.

Materials Needed:
- Excuse strips from the Excuses...Excuses Activity sheet copied and cut apart
- Pencils

Procedures:
1. **Introduction:** Ask: *Have you ever not really wanted to do something or it was hard to do so you made up an excuse so you didn't have to do it?* Allow students to share giving examples. Ask: *How about school? What are some excuses people come up with about school.*

2. Explain to the students that you need their help to rewrite the negative excuse statements/thoughts to positive statements/thoughts. Hand each student several cut out excuse statements from the Excuses...Excuses Activity Sheet and ask them to help that person find a more positive way to think about the situation and write it in the space provided. Students may work individually or in pairs. Take turns sharing statements and discussing with the group.

3. **Closure:** Ask students to think about excuses they may make during the week. Challenge the students to be aware of the excuse and to rewrite/rethink the excuse to a positive statement or thought.

Excuses...Excuses Activity Sheet

Directions: Copy and cut out the excuse slips. Rewrite these negative thoughts to positive thoughts. Share and discuss these with the group.

---

1. I'll never use that subject so why should I study it.

---

2. This junk is too hard, I'll never learn it, so why try?

---

3. My teacher didn't explain it well.

---

4. The test was too hard.

---

5. I can't do it.

---

6. It got lost.

---

7. Mom forgot to sign it.

---

8. My teacher doesn't like me.

---

9. I'll just sit here until someone notices I'm not working.

---

10. I don't know what the word means, so I just won't do any of it.

POST ASSESSMENT ACTIVITY C 7
Fill in the Blanks to School Success

Purpose: To summarize school success skills and to evaluate the progress of the group through post assessments.

Materials Needed:
- Chart paper and marker
- Student Post Assessment Form copied for each student
- Parent/Teacher Post Assessment Form copied for each student

Procedures:
1. **Introduction**: Ask students to think back to the different school success skills and strategies that have been discussed in the group. Share and review this information.

2. Introduce the Fill in the Blank review activity. Choose a phrase from a skill or strategy that has been discussed in your group. (Use phrases such as: "Use your de-magnetizing button to avoid a problem." "Get organized." "Schedule in a time for homework." "Plan ahead for long range assignments." "Use flash cards to help prepare for a test." "Use your stress ball to manage test stress." "Make sure to follow directions." "Maintain a positive attitude about school." Use the phrases of the activities/skills you have talked about in the group). On the chart paper draw blank lines for the phrase – one line for each letter with a space between the words and add punctuation. Students can take turns selecting a letter. If the letter is a letter from the designated phrase then add the letter to the chart. If it is not then write the letter to the side to remind others that the letter has been called. Continue on until a student guesses the phrase. As a review ask questions, elaborate, and discuss the importance of the phrase. Then select another phrase and continue.

3. Ask students to complete the Student Post Assessment Form. Allow students to share information from their forms if they choose. Send out and collect the Parent/Teacher Post Assessment.

4. **Closure:** Celebrate the group, the time together, and point out their successes. Encourage others to do the same. Encourage group members to continue to work on their school success skills.

   Follow-up: Follow up with students individually, consulting with their teachers, and/or sending notes to the students to encourage and compliment. Consider scheduling a monthly support group.

Student Post Assessment For School Success

Name: _____

Directions: Complete the post assessment. Mark your answers honestly.

	STRONGLY AGREE	AGREE	DISAGREE	STRONGLY DISAGREE
1. I behave well in class.	4	3	2	1
2. I stay focused and listen carefully in class	4	3	2	1
3. I am organized.	4	3	2	1
4. I know how to study and learn material.	4	3	2	1
5. I complete my homework efficiently.	4	3	2	1
6. I know how to take tests.	4	3	2	1
7. I have a good attitude about school.	4	3	2	1

8. In School Success Skills group I learned: _____

_____

9. The most helpful part of the group was: _____

_____

10. I would recommend to include the following in the School Success Skills group in the future: _____

_____

_____

PARENT/TEACHER NOTE
Post Assessment

Dear Parent/Teacher,

We are concluding our small group on School Success Skills that your child has been a participant. We have focused on the skills of:

Please continue to reinforce these skills as your child works to do their best and be successful. I have enjoyed working with your child and will continue to follow up with him/her during the year. To help assess the degree to which your child is implementing the skills learned, please complete the post assessment listed below and return. Your answers need to reflect your child's present behavior.

Sincerely,

Your Child's Counselor

PARENT/TEACHER NEEDS ASSESSMENT FOR

STUDENT/CHILD'S NAME _____

	STRONGLY AGREE	AGREE	DISAGREE	STRONGLY DISAGREE
1. He/she behaves well in class.	4	3	2	1
2. He/she stays focused and listen carefully in class	4	3	2	1
3. He/she is organized.	4	3	2	1
4. He/she knows how to study and learn material.	4	3	2	1
5. He/she completes my homework efficiently.	4	3	2	1
6. He/she knows how to take tests.	4	3	2	1
7. He/she has a good attitude about school.	4	3	2	1

Comments:

Self Concept

Self-Concept

Building and maintaining a positive self-concept is important in being a happy, production person. Self-concept, feeling good about who you are, can't depend on outside events or other people – of only having good things happen to us or in depending on others to tell us how good we are. Self-concept must be developed from the inside. We must acknowledge that we are all lovable and capable people, appreciate our strengths and the things we can do well, and develop positive thoughts and skills to deal with life when things do not go "right".

Small group counseling on self-concept offers the opportunity to acknowledge strengths and positive qualities, to learn to manage negative thinking, and to build on positive characteristics. So much of our outlook on life is rooted in our own perception of ourselves and our abilities. Through small groups, the perception of the students can be explored, areas of weakness targeted and strengthened, and skills learned about how to focus on the positives. Information in this book is provided for you to first assess and determine your group's specific needs and then for you to choose skill building activities from the multiple list that best meets the needs of your group. The first activity in this section Puzzling Pieces is a needs assessment activity that collects feedback from the student, teacher, and parent. Once the specific needs of your group are determined then you can use the Correlation Chart on page 244 to select session activities. The Small Group Roster and Planning Form on pages 19-20 can be helpful in writing down the group plans. For each session a main skill building activity needs to be selected as well as an icebreakers/energizer chosen (See Icebreakers/Energizers Section). An additional, optional component can be added to each group session – Service Learning (See the Service Learning Section for more information).

This book is designed in hopes of helping counselors to be focused on students' needs and to be efficient and effective in helping students.

Self - Concept

• INITIAL GROUP SESSION...

Review the Getting Started: First Group Session on page 17. Complete the Needs Assessment Activity D which includes a student and a parent/teacher needs assessment. Review the areas of need from these assessments and with the use of the Needs Assessment Correlation to Self-Concept Skill Building Activities Chart on page 244, plan the skill building activities for the remaining group sessions.

• SKILL BUILDING ACTIVITIES ...

The following is a list of self-concept skill building activities grouped by sub topics that relate to the needs assessment. Each activity will take about 20-25 minutes therefore only one activity needs to be planned for each group meeting. Not all activities will be used, only those that relate to the needs of your group. Select your activities, guided by your Needs Assessment Correlation to Self-Concept Skill Building Activities Chart on page 244. You may also want to use the Small Group Roster and Planning Chart on pages 19-20 to organize your sessions and activities.

• CLOSING GROUP SESSION...

Review the How to End: Final Group Session on page 23. Complete the Closing Group Activity D4 which includes a student and a parent/teacher post assessment. Use this information to evaluate the group and to determine follow up with individual students on continuing weaknesses.

NEEDS ASSESSMENT ACTIVITY D
Puzzling Pieces

Purpose: To assess the needs of the students in the group as they relate to self concept.

Materials Needed:
• Copy of the IALAC sign from the Puzzling Pieces Activity sheet
• Copy of the puzzle IALAC sign from the Puzzling Pieces activity sheet, cut apart and placed in a plastic bag labeled "IALAC Repair Kit"
• Tape
• Student Needs Assessment copied for each student
• Parent/Teacher Needs Assessment copied for each parent/teacher of the students

Procedures:
1. **Introduction:** Display the IALAC sign and explain that the letters stand for 'I Am Lovable and Capable'*. Elaborate that we are all lovable and capable, giving different examples of what makes us so. Explain that we all carry an IALAC sign around with us except that our sign is invisible – it's there but it just can't be seen like a piece of paper, yet we see and feel it in different ways. Sometimes our sign is big and sometimes it gets pretty small depending on how loved and capable we feel. However, our sign will never go away because we will always be lovable and capable. Ask students to share what a person who feels loved and capable might be saying or doing. Summarize their responses and then ask what a person who doesn't feel very loved or capable might be doing or saying.

2. Share with the students the following story:

   I have a story to tell today of a friend named Samantha (or substitute any other name). She had one of those terrible, awful, no good, very bad days. Her IALAC sign got torn into different pieces with not much left. By the end of her day she was not feeling very loved and capable. Let's listen in to the story.

   (Ask the help of a volunteer to hold the IALAC sign. At different places in the story as indicated, tear a piece of the sign off. By the end of the story only a small piece of the sign needs to be left.)

   It was a regular school morning and Samantha's alarm clock was ringing its time to get out of bed. Samantha thought to herself 'I'll sleep for just two more minutes and then I'll get up.' Well as it happened the two minutes turned into twenty and when she finally woke and got out of bed she was late for school. She thought to herself, 'I'm so dumb, I can't even get up in the mornings when I'm supposed to.' (tear off a piece of the sign)

   She arrived at school late, went by the office to get a pass, and then on to class. When she got to class they were already busy doing their morning work. Samantha quickly put her books up and began the assignment. The assignment was to practice cursive handwriting. Samantha was excited about learning her cursive and she wanted it to be perfect. She was writing her letters well until it came to the letter b in cursive and it just didn't look right so she erased it and tried again, and erased it and tried again, and erased it and tried again. She just didn't want to turn in that paper unless all of her letters were perfect. Well that letter b just wouldn't look right so she crammed her paper into her desk and thought to herself, 'I just can't turn that paper in when I did such a terrible job.'
   (tear off another piece of paper)

continued

After the morning assignment, the class worked on spelling and reading. Class was going fine until it was time to do math – they were studying fractions in math. Samantha hated doing fractions because they were so hard for her. She thought to herself, 'I won't even try – I can't ever get math.' (tear another piece of paper). Later that morning they were taking a bathroom break and wouldn't you know it but Samantha got stuck in line next to one of the most popular girls who picks on people that aren't in her crowd. The girl looked at Samantha and said, 'What happened to your hair this morning did you forget to brush it?' Samantha felt horrible, she just hung her head down and tried to smooth her hair down with her hand. (tear another piece of paper).

Samantha made it through the rest of the morning and it was time for lunch. Samantha was standing in line, picked up her lunch tray, went to the lunch lady who takes the money. When she reached into her pocket for her lunch money there was none there. Samantha figured she must have forgotten to get it from the kitchen table this morning when she was in such a hurry running late. She felt embarrassed about her mistake. The lunch lady was nice and she said just to remember to bring it tomorrow. Samantha thought to herself, 'That was so dumb of me to forget that money, mom reminded me to get it this morning but I still forgot it." (tear another piece of paper). Samantha sat and ate her lunch and then her class went out for recess. Samantha was feeling so down about her day that she didn't want to play with any of her friends so she just sat on the bench by herself. Even when her best friend invited her to play she told her no.
(tear another piece of paper)

Samantha made it through the rest of the day at school without anything too bad happening. She rode the bus home, went inside, and sunk onto the couch in the den. She thought about what a terrible day it had been and she thought about how she can't seem to do anything right. (tear another piece of paper) While she was sitting on the couch the phone rang. It was her friend down the street who had just gotten a new skateboard. She asked Samantha to come down and try it out but she said 'No, thanks.' She thought to herself 'I'm never good at trying new things and I don't want to embarrass myself.' (tear another piece of paper)

Samantha watched TV, ate supper, finished her homework and went to bed. When her mom was saying good night to her, she told her a little about her day. Her mom said, "Samantha, we all have days when things go wrong but you are a wonderful, capable person who can do so many things well and who can learn to handle the things that don't go so well in a good way. Get a good night's sleep and tomorrow's another day.

3. Briefly discuss the story asking if any of them have ever had days like that. Ask them what they can relate to in the story. Summarize and connect each others' stories.

4. Bring out the bag marked IALAC Repair Kit. Tell the students that you do have a repair kit that may help Samantha handle those problems in a positive way. As the items are drawn, read, and discussed, relate how that specific skill could be of help to Samantha in the story. Also hand each student a Needs Assessment Sheet. Explain that as the items from the repair kit are discussed, they need to locate the same number item on their sheet and circle the answer that indicates to what extent they have that self-concept skill. Let students know that you will use this information to let you know what skill areas we need to learn and practice in group to be of help. As the pieces of paper from the repair kit are pulled from the bag and discussed, place the

continued

piece of paper on the table and as more pieces are added put the IALAC puzzle back together. When all pieces are in place – add some tape to finish the repair job.

5. **Closure:** Encourage students to remind themselves that they are always lovable and capable even when things don't go just right.

Explain to the students that you have a similar assessment for their parent and/or teacher to complete. Send copies with the students to give to their Parent/Teacher to complete and return. Or you may choose to put the Needs Assessment in teachers' boxes and mail to parents.

Refer to the Needs Assessment Correlation to Skill Building Activities Chart for Self-Concept to assist in planning group sessions. Select an appropriate skill building activity for each session depending on the needs determined from the assessments as well as group discussions and observations.

*I Am Lovable and Capable concept was originally developed by Dr. Sid Simon.

Puzzling Pieces Activity Sheet

Directions: Copy the IALAC sign.

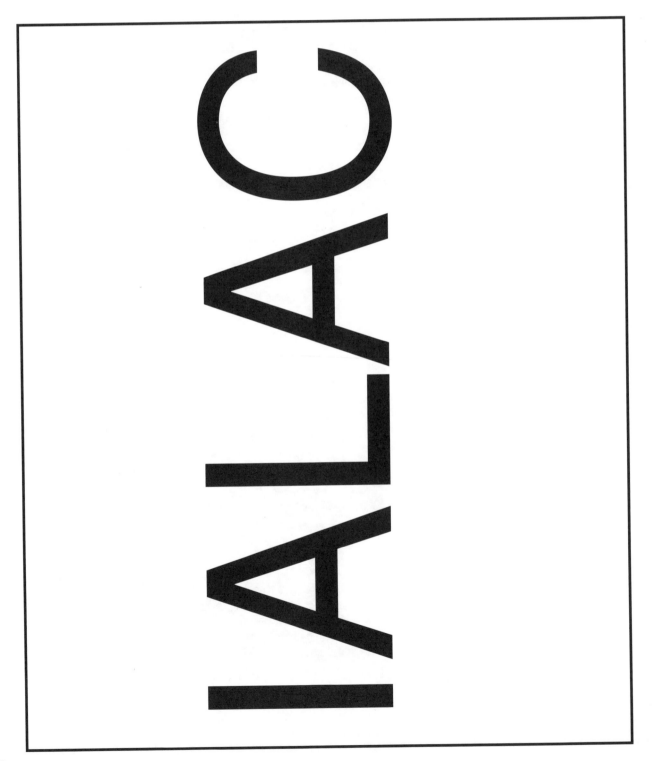

Puzzling Pieces Activity Sheet

Directions: Copy the puzzle IALAC sign. Create an IALAC repair kit from the puzzle IALAC sign by cutting apart the puzzle pieces and placing them in a plastic bag. Label the bag, "IALAC Repair Kit."

I can have a positive thought even if things are not perfect

I know and appreciate the good things about me and the things I can do well.

I can think positively even if I get criticized or teased by others.

I have the skills to build on my strengths to maintain a strong self-image.

I can think positively even if things are difficult or hard.

I can think positively even if I make a mistake or things don't go quite right.

I have the skills to speak up for myself and the courage to try new things.

I have the skills to manage my feelings in a positive way.

STUDENT NEEDS ASSESSMENT
for Self-Concept

Name: _____

Directions: Complete the needs assessment as directed in the Puzzling Pieces Activity procedure Step 4. Mark your answers honestly. The information will be collected and used by the group leader to plan learning activities for the group based on the needs.

	STRONGLY AGREE	AGREE	DISAGREE	STRONGLY DISAGREE
1. I know and appreciate the good things about me and the things I can do well.	4	3	2	1
2. I can handle it even if things are not perfect.	4	3	2	1
3. I can think positively even if things are difficult or hard.	4	3	2	1
4. I can think positively even if I get criticized or teased by others.	4	3	2	1
5 . I can think positively even if I make a mistake or things don't go quite right.	4	3	2	1
6. I have the skills to manage my feelings in a positive way.	4	3	2	1
7. I have the skills to build on my strengths to maintain a strong self-image.	4	3	2	1
8. I have the skills to speak up for myself and the courage to try new things.	4	3	2	1

PARENT/TEACHER NOTE
Needs Assessment

Dear Parent/Teacher,

Building and maintaining a positive self-concept is important in being a happy, productive person. Self-concept, feeling good about who you are, can't depend on outside events or other people – of only having good things happen to us or in depending on others to tell us how good we are. Self-concept must be developed from the inside. We must acknowledge that we are all lovable and capable people, appreciate our strengths and the things we can do well, and then develop positive thoughts and skills to handle when things don't go 'right'. In small group we will be addressing these skill areas.

In order to structure our self-concept small group to meet the specific needs of the group members we need your input. Review your child's skills and thoughts relating to self-concept. Complete the needs assessment given below and return. Please feel free to add comments or to share any information that would be helpful as we begin our small group. Thank you for your input as we work together to help our students be their best.

Sincerely,

Your Child's Counselor

PARENT/TEACHER NEEDS ASSESSMENT FOR

STUDENT/CHILD'S NAME _____

	STRONGLY AGREE	AGREE	DISAGREE	STRONGLY DISAGREE
1. He/she knows and appreciates the good things about himself/herself and the things he/she can do well.	4	3	2	1
2. He/she can handle it even if things are not perfect.	4	3	2	1
3. He/she can think positively even if things are difficult or hard.	4	3	2	1
4. He/she can think positively even if he/she gets criticized or teased by others.	4	3	2	1
5 . He/she can think positively even if he/she makes a mistake or things don't go quite right.	4	3	2	1
6. He/she has the skills to manage his/her feelings in a positive way.	4	3	2	1
7. He/she has the skills to build on his/her strengths to maintain a strong self-image.	4	3	2	1
8. He/she has the skills to speak up for himself/herself and the courage to try new things.	4	3	2	1

Comments:

NEEDS ASSESSMENT CORRELATION TO
Self-Concept Skill Building Activities

Directions: Use the chart to assist in planning skill building activities for group sessions. Below is a listing of the activities as they relate to each statement in the needs assessments. Select an appropriate skill building activity for each session depending on the needs determined from the assessments as well as group discussions and observations. Area of needs may be indicated by a score of "1" or "2" on an item on the assessment. For an area of heavy need you may choose to plan for several sessions utilizing several skill building activities focusing on that sub topic. For lighter needs you may choose only one session choosing only one skill building activity from that sub topic. If there is no need indicated for that sub topic then do not plan to use a skill building activity from that area. Remember these skill building activities are written covering a wide range of information so that you may choose only the ones that fit the group's needs. All activities will not be used in a typical 6-8 session group. Note that most skill building activities for self-concept are marked by the letter D indicating this section of the book, however at times a skill building activity in another section will be referenced and will be indicated by a different section letter.

NEEDS ASSESSMENT STATEMENTS

Statement				
1. I know and appreciate the good things about me and the things I can do well.	D1.1	D1.2	D1.3	B1.1
2. I can handle it even if things are not perfect.	D2.1	A5.2		
3. I can think positively even if things are difficult or hard.	D2.2	A5.1		A6.1
4. I can think positively even if I get criticized or teased by others.	D2.3	B5.1	A4.1	
5 . I can think positively even if I make a mistake or things don't go quite right.	D2.4	D2.5	A7.1	
6. I have the skills to manage my feelings in a positive way.	D3.1			
7. I have the skills to build on my strengths to maintain a strong self-image.	D3.2	D3.3		
8. I have the skills to speak up for myself and the courage to try new things.	D3.4	B2.1	B2.2	B2.3

SKILL BUILDING ACTIVITIES

ACTIVITY D1.1
Thumbprint

Purpose: To emphasize each person's uniqueness and individual strengths.

Materials Needed:
- Copy for each student of the Thumbprint activity sheet
- Washable ink pad for thumbprints and wet paper towels to clean up
- Pencils, pens, markers

Procedures:

1. **Introduction:** Ask: *Have you ever met anyone similar to you – that is good at the same things you are or likes the same things that you do?* Allow for answers and sharing. Ask: *About how many people have you ever met? Have you ever met anyone who is <u>exactly</u> like you?* Come to the conclusion that out of the many, many people you have met and out of the millions and trillions of people in the world that there is no one just like you.

2. Introduce the word unique. Explain that unique means one of a kind – no one just like you. Take a moment to consider how awesome it is to realize out of the millions and trillions of people in the world there is no one else just like you. Share that no one can ever take their place - each person is needed and it makes each person special. Elaborate that everybody has different strengths and weaknesses and that we are all good at different things. Some may be good at learning math more easily, some are good at sports, some are good listeners, some are good at helping others, some have musical talent, etc.

3. Direct students to examine their thumbprint and the thumbprint of the person sitting next to them. Point out that this is the physical evidence that each person is unique for each thumbprint is different – different in the pattern and the swirl of the lines. Provide each person with a Thumbprint Activity sheet. Instruct the students to press their thumb on the washable ink pad and then place their thumb in the center of their paper to leave their thumbprint. Provide wet paper towels to clean their thumb. Have students compare their prints.

4. Review the areas on the sheet for the students to answer and allow time for them to complete their sheet. Allow each person to share the information on their sheets sharing their strengths and uniqueness. You may choose to have them act out the things they are good at and have other students guess. Compliment and encourage each student as they share emphasizing their uniqueness and importance.

5. **Closure:** Encourage students to focus on their strengths and be proud of themselves.

Thumbprint Activity Sheet

Directions: Copy for each student to complete. Using a washable ink pad, students need to add their thumbprint to the center of the sheet.

I know how to....

At school I am good at....

At home I am good at....

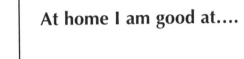

_____'s Thumbprint

With my friends I like to....

With my friends I like to....

Something I am able to do that may be hard for others my age to do is...

An activity I enjoying doing is...

ACTIVITY D1.2
I'm A Star!

Purpose: To allow students a chance to share the good things about themselves and to learn about each other.

Materials Needed:
- Copy of I'm A Star Activity sheet for each student and one extra
- Dice
- Pencils

Procedures:

1. **Introduction:** Discuss the beauty of a night's sky when the stars are out. Point out how each star is different – different shapes, sizes, brightness – and yet each star is beautiful adding to the beauty of the other stars. Relate the stars in the sky to each person being a star adding their own beauty or strengths and talents with others.

2. Hand each student a copy of the I'm A Star Activity sheet and place one copy in the middle of the group. Explain to the students the I'm A Star game as follows: Each student takes turns rolling the dice. The student is to answer the statement on the number on the point of the star that corresponds to the number on the roll of the dice. The student needs to share their answer with the whole group while the group listens well. Then the student needs to write down their answer on that point of the star. If a player rolls a number that they have already shared then they lose that turn. Point out to the students that number six roll is to repeat something that someone else has shared about themselves in group; therefore, stress the importance of listening as others share. If they are unable to complete the answer to number six then they must pass and try again later. (If for some reason a player has difficulty answering other statements they may call on someone else to help them. If the other person is successful in helping them then allow the other person to add a plus on their star.) Continue until a player or all players complete their star. Explain that all are winners because of the good things they have to share with others.

3. **Closure:** Allow students to take their stars with them to remind them of their bright talents and skills. Encourage students to add to their stars during the week.

I'm A Star Activity Sheet

Directions: Need a dice and a copy for each student. Follow the game directions given in Procedures Step 2.

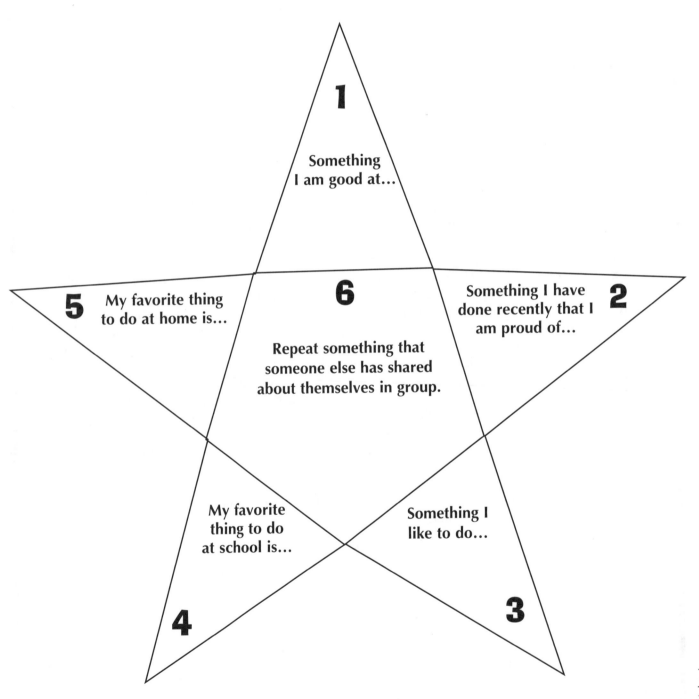

1

Something
I am good at...

5 My favorite thing
to do at home is...

6

Repeat something that
someone else has shared
about themselves in group.

Something I have
done recently that I
am proud of...

2

My favorite
thing to do
at school is...

Something I
like to do...

4

3

ACTIVITY D1.3
The Mirror's Reflection

Purpose: To stress the importance of how your good qualities and characteristics on the inside are more important than how you look on the outside.

Materials Needed:
- Foil and a copy of The Mirror's Reflection Activity Sheet for each student. Cut a foil circle to cover the mirror part on each student's activity sheet. Attach the foil to the top part of the mirror with tape or staples allowing the foil part to be lifted.
- Hand held mirror
- Chart paper and markers
- Pencils

Procedures:
1. **Introduction:** Hold a mirror in front of each student and ask them to share what they see. Ask: *Is how you look on the outside – your hair, eyes, etc. - the true you? Where/how do you find the true you?* Encourage students to talk guiding them to the true person is the kind of person they are on the inside – their qualities and good characteristics.

2. Explain that we need a special mirror that looks beyond just the outside of a person – one that looks at the kind of person they truly are on the inside. Begin brainstorming a list and writing on chart paper different good qualities and characteristics of people. Include such words as: kind, helpful, organized, brave, honest, respectful, loyal, loving, dependable, cooperative, polite, understanding, fair, intelligent, talented, cheerful, athletic, caring, responsible, team player, self disciplined, trustworthy, etc.

3. Hand each student The Mirror's Reflection Activity sheet. Ask students to think about the kind of person they are. Instruct them to select any of the good qualities and characteristics from the group list and write on the outside of the mirror outline on their sheet. Have students share this with the group.

4. Next ask them to think about important people in their lives such as their mom, dad, brother, sister, grandparent, aunt or uncle, teacher, neighbor, etc. and to lift the foil and write their name in the mirror under the foil. Next ask them to think for a moment how they would guess that person sees them – guess as to which positive quality or characteristic that other person may say describes them. Write that positive word beside their name. Have students share this with the group.

5. Ask students to take their mirror sheet with them and during the week talk to the important people in their lives and ask them to choose a word on the outside of their mirror that they think best describes you. Check to see if you guessed the right word that they would say. If not, add the word.

6. **Closure:** The kind of person we are on the inside is more important than how we look on the outside. Encourage the students to appreciate their good qualities and to continue to be the best

The Mirror's Reflection Activity Sheet

Directions: For each student copy and add a foil circle over the mirror section. Use tape or staples to attach the foil at the top allowing for the bottom to be lifted. Use the activity sheet as directed in Procedure Step 3, 4 and 5.

Name

ACTIVITY D2.1
It Has to be Perfect!

Purpose: To explore the feelings and thoughts behind perfectionism and to refocus on realistic goals.

Materials Needed:
- Copy of the picture on It Has to be Perfect! Activity Sheet
- Chart paper and marker

Procedures:

1. **Introduction:** Open a discussion about perfection by asking: *What does it mean to be perfect? How does it feel when a person is trying to be perfect? Why do you think people try to be perfect?* Explore the possibility that people think their value and self worth depend on doing things perfectly. Ask students what the error is in that thinking. Ask: *What happens when perfection is not reached?* Explore the feelings and frustrations that go along with trying to be perfect.

2. Show the group the picture from the It Has to be Perfect! Activity sheet of "Perfect Polly" as you tell the following:

   Perfect Polly is a person who thinks she has to have everything perfect. When she is practicing her writing and one of her letters is not perfect she erases and tries again, then erases and tries again, and erases... All the time she seems to focus on what's wrong with her paper instead of what's right. When she is writing a creative story, I hear Polly making moaning sounds and crumpling up her paper and throwing it away. I think that Polly feels that if she doesn't get her work just perfect then she must be a dumb person who is worthless. Out at recess, when we play games together Polly gets real mad real easy if someone doesn't play the game just right. Polly seems to be frustrated and upset a lot. Sometimes I'm scared to be around her because I don't want her to get mad at me. Can you help her?

3. After the story tell the students that she needs our advice. Ask: *What do you think Polly needs to say to herself or to think in order to help her deal with things better?* Write their advice on chart paper.

4. Ask for a volunteer to pretend they are a toddler first learning to walk – taking their first steps. (May take turns having several role-play). If they realistically role played the first steps, they probably were very shaky and perhaps fell but got back up. Explain that even though a toddler does not walk perfectly when he/she begins, the toddler usually does not give up. Next ask the same student(s) to walk across the room like they usually do today. Process how that student probably had trouble learning to walk at first when he/she was a toddler and probably made some mistakes but that it doesn't seem to have affected his/her ability to walk today. It would have only affected it if he/she had given up.

continued

5. Write the word "goal" on chart paper. Define the word as the target area or the point that you want to get to. Share that it's important to set goals but the goals must be realistic. An example of an unrealistic goal is for the toddler who has never walked before to think, "Hey, I'm going to get up, run across the room and do a few jumping jacks." We too can set some unrealistic goals for ourselves that can cause disappointment and frustration. Ask the students to think back to the information shared about Polly. Ask them to point out any unrealistic goals that Polly had. (every letter has to be written perfectly, every sentence has to be perfect on the rough draft of a creative writing story, everybody has to play the right way – how I want them to.) Encourage students to share other unrealistic goals that we may set for ourselves. Help each other refocus to a more realistic goal.

6. **Closure:** Ask students during the week to do a reality check and make sure their own daily goals and expectations are realistic.

It Has to be Perfect! Activity Sheet

Directions: Copy and show the picture of Perfect Polly as you share her story given in Procedure Step 2.

ACTIVITY D2.2
I Can't Do This – It's Too Hard!

Purpose: To encourage students to use determination, perseverance, and a positive attitude to overcome difficulties.

Materials Needed:
- Story book, *Wilma Unlimited* by Kroll
- Five sheets of plain paper and scissors
- Chart paper and marker

Procedures:

1. **Introduction:** Ask the students to share with the group something that is hard to do or is difficult for them. Write these on chart paper.

2. Explain that there are many times when we think things are impossible. Show the piece of paper and ask the students if they think you can cut a hole in the paper that's large enough to pass your whole body through. If the students think they can do it, allow a few to try. Discuss how this seems almost impossible and then demonstrate how you can do it using the following steps:
   - Fold the paper in half (square or rectangle).
   - Cut in a straight line from fold to open edges – but not all the way – at both ends.
   - Continue to cut strips all the way across, alternating open edges to fold then fold to open edges – but DO NOT cut all the way down.
   - Cut along the fold – EXCEPT 2 outer strips.
   - Open and step through the hole.
   Discuss how sometimes things we think are impossible are really possible, we just have to find a different way to do them.

3. Tell the students that you want to read an inspirational story to them of a person, Wilma, who overcame difficulty to succeed. Read the story, *Wilma Unlimited*. It is the story of a young child who became physically disabled from childhood polio and yet with her determination and perseverance became a three time Olympic gold medalist in track. Discuss the story, pointing out how Wilma's determination, perseverance, and "I can" attitude led to her success.

4. Refer back to the chart of difficulties generated at the beginning of the group. Ask the students to share a way to persevere and have an "I can" attitude with each of those difficulties. Point out that they may have to look at it in a different way, or they may need to ask others for help or support.

5. **Closure:** Challenge the students to work hard to overcome those things that are hard or difficult for them. Encourage them to check out the difficult stories of the following people: Abraham Lincoln, Tom Dempsey, Jackie Robinson, Ludwig Van Beethoven, Helen Keller, Thomas Alva Edison, Albert Einstein, Lou Ferrigno, Bessie Coleman, Harriet Tubman, Agatha Christie, or Tom Cruise.

ACTIVITY D2.3
They Said I'm No Good

Purpose: To help students counteract others' teasing and criticizing by realizing the difference between fact and opinion. Students are encouraged to make good choices about whose opinion to value and to focus on thinking positively.

Materials Needed:
• Copy and cut apart the statements on the They Said I'm No Good Activity sheet
• pencils

Procedures:

1. **Introduction:** Ask: *How might someone **feel** when they are being teased or criticized? What might someone **think** when they are being teased or criticized?* Explore with the students that how we think about something affects how we feel so it's important to focus on positive thinking when being teased or criticized.

2. Ask: *Because someone says to a person that they are dumb, does it mean that it is true – that it is a fact?* Ask: *What is the difference between FACT ad OPNION?* Discuss that a fact is something that can be proved and is an accepted truth. While an opinion is a belief or statement based on one's own judgment rather than on certain knowledge. Encourage students to evaluate what someone says. If the teasing statement is based on someone's opinion rather than fact then simply take it as an opinion. Encourage students to make good choices about whose opinion to value. Encourage students to think positively of themselves and their abilities and to have high opinions of themselves.

3. Copy and cut apart the statements on the They Said I'm No Good Activity Sheet. Distribute to each student a statement. Tell the students to read their statement, mark whether the statement is FACT or OPINION, and then write a positive way to think about the statement. Allow students to share and discuss their statement and answers.

4. **Closure:** Encourage students to evaluate what others say, decide if there is any truth to the teasing statements and to think positively.

They Said I'm No Good Activity Sheet

Directions: Copy and cut along the dotted lines. Circle either FACT or OPINION and then write a positive thought to counteract the statement.

Your hair is red!	**FACT? or OPINION?** Positive thought: _____ _____ _____ _____
You don't know anything.	**FACT? or OPINION?** Positive thought: _____ _____ _____ _____
You can't do anything right.	**FACT? or OPINION?** Positive thought: _____ _____ _____ _____
Your clothes are ugly.	**FACT? or OPINION?** Positive thought: _____ _____ _____ _____
You're short!	**FACT? or OPINION?** Positive thought: _____ _____ _____ _____
I'm taller than you are!	**FACT? or OPINION?** Positive thought: _____ _____ _____ _____

ACTIVITY D2.4
Frame It!

Purpose: To help students see difficult situations in a positive way.

Materials Needed:
- Copy on heavy paper and cut out the picture frames on the Frame It! Activity Sheet
- Copy and cut out the eight picture situations
- Blank paper for each student
- Pencils, markers, etc.
- Two copies of the same picture: one framed in an old, worn out frame and the other picture framed in a nice frame

Procedures:
1. **Introduction:** Show a picture framed with an old torn up picture frame, then show the same picture in a nice frame. Ask which one looks the best – the old frame or the nice frame. Most people would choose the one with the nice frame. Point out that it is the same picture in both but the way you choose to frame it can help or hurt the picture.

2. Relate that this can be true of life. How we choose to look at a situation – the frame we put on it - can help the situation or make it worse. Hold up the two frames from the Frame It! Activity sheet. Have students read and discuss the messages of each frame. Tell the students that you are going to share some situations with them and that you need their help to frame the situation with both negative and positive thoughts. Use the prepared frames and situations. First show the negative frame and ask the students what negative things a person might be thinking and feeling if that was the picture. Then, using the same situation change to the positive frame. Ask them to share a positive way they could look at that situation. Continue practicing reframing the different situations given.

3. Give each student a blank sheet of paper and instruct them to draw or write a situation of their own that needs reframing. Allow students to take turns adding the frames around their pictures and getting help from the group on a positive way to think about the situation

4. **Closure:** Encourage students to carry their invisible positive frames around with them to reframe difficult situations in a positive way.

Frame It! Activity Sheet

Directions: Copy on heavy paper and cut out the two picture frames – don't forget to cut out the center of the frames. Copy and cut out the eight pictures on the following pages. In group, take turns putting both frames around each picture situation. First show the negative frame and ask the students what negative things a person might be thinking and feeling if that was the frame. Then, using the same situation change to the positive frame. Ask them to share a positive way they could look at that situation. Continue practicing reframing the different situations given.

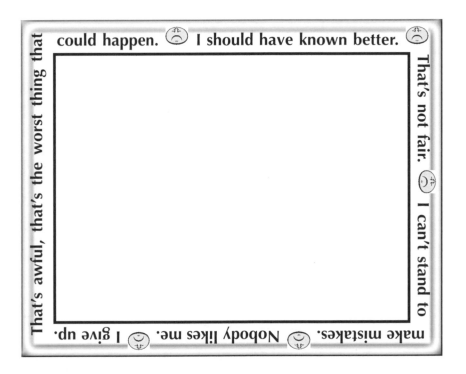

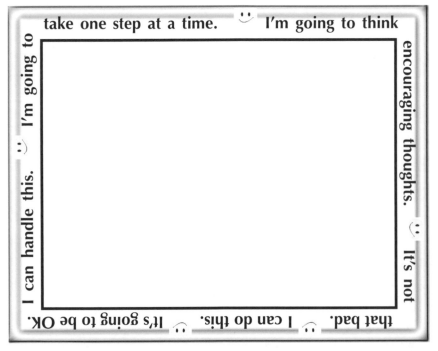

Frame It! Activity Sheet

You didn't get invited
to a skating party.

You got a bad haircut
that looks ugly.

You got a bad
grade on a paper.

You didn't get what you
wanted for your birthday.

Frame It! Activity Sheet

Your friend went off and played with someone else at recess

Your parent wouldn't let you go to the movies with your friends.

You wanted to answer the question but the teacher didn't call on you in class.

You are having difficulty learning fractions in math class.

ACTIVITY D2.5
Garbage vs. Recycled Thoughts

Purpose: To help students distinguish between positive and negative thoughts and to help rewrite the negative thoughts to positive thoughts.

Materials Needed:
- The following statements written on sentence strips:
  - I'll never learn to divide!
  - I hate reading this book.
  - This word is really hard to sound out, but if I keep working, I'll figure it out.
  - This picture I drew is really ugly.
  - I did my best on the Accelerated Reader test even though I didn't get all the questions right.
  - Nobody likes me.
  - Even though I don't have as many friends as Jamie, I have a few really great friends.
  - It's not fair that I can't have clothes like my friends do.
  - I'll never be popular.
  - My teacher never calls on me to do anything special for her like she does other kids.
  - If I keep showing how responsible I can be, someone is bound to notice.
- Copy of the Garbage vs. Recycling Activity sheet for each student. Cut the sheets in half, dividing the garbage thought from the recycled thought.
- Garbage can and recycling bin if available – if not draw a picture on chart paper
- Paper shredder

Procedures:
1. **Introduction:** Show a garbage can and ask students the following: *What is garbage? What do you do with garbage? Can garbage be recycled? How? Do you ever eat garbage? Why not? What might happen if you did eat garbage?* Explain to the students that sometimes people put garbage thoughts in their own heads. For example, they talk to themselves and say things like, "I can't do this," "I'm stupid," "This is awful," or "I can't stand this." Explain how such negative thoughts become "garbage" for the mind, how they use a lot of negative energy, and how these thoughts get in the way of doing positive things. Point out that if we keep these "garbage" thoughts in our head they can make us mentally unhealthy or sick.

2. Show a recycling bin. Discuss recycling. Explain that when you recycle you take "trash" and make it into something useful. When you have a "garbage" thought, you can recycle that garbage thought by asking yourself some questions: Can I change this? If so, how? If not, what can I do to make the most of the situation.

3. Using the prepared sentence strips, take turns for the students to decide if it is a garbage thought or a recycled thought. Place the sentence strips in or beside the garbage can if it is a garbage thought and beside the recycling bin if it is a recycled thought. Discuss the situations and if it is a garbage thought discuss how the thought could be rewritten to a recycled thought.

continued

4. Hand each student the Garbage Thought half sheet from the Garbage vs. Recycled Thoughts Activity sheet. Have each student write a garbage thought they have about themselves. Instruct them to come up one at a time and to send that thought through the paper shredder and get rid of that unhealthy thought.

5. Hand each student the Recycled Thought half sheet from the Garbage vs. Recycled Thoughts Activity sheet, have each student write a recycled thought of that garbage thought. Have them keep this one.

6. **Closure:** Encourage the students during the week to check their thinking and to change any garbage thoughts to recycled thoughts.

Note: This activity was adapted with permission from *Classroom Guidance Activities* (1997) by Wittmer, Thompson, & Loesch. Minneapolis, MN: Educational Media Corp.

Garbage vs. Recycled Thoughts Activity Sheet

My garbage thought: _____

_____

_____

_____

_____

_____

_____

_____

My recycled thought:_____

_____

_____

_____

_____

_____

_____

_____

ACTIVITY D3.1
Penny for Your Thoughts

Purpose: To maintain positive thoughts about all kinds of feelings.

Materials Needed:
- Copy of the Penny for Your Thoughts Game sheet
- Penny for each student
- Chart paper and marker

Procedures:

1. **Introduction:** Hold up a penny and ask them if they have ever heard the following saying and what do they think it means: " Penny For Your Thoughts". Explain that we want to focus on our feeling thoughts – of how to handle all kinds of feelings in a positive way.

2. Make a list on chart paper of different feeling words that we typically experience. Make sure to include both pleasant and unpleasant feeling words.

3. Next prepare a Penny for Your Thoughts Game card by having the group select 16 of their top feeling words from their list. Write these 16 words, 1 per square, on the Penny For Your Thoughts Game sheet. Give each word a point value somewhere between 5 and 15 and write the number beside the feeling word in the square. Hand each student a penny and explain the rules of the game as follows: *Points are awarded if the student successfully tosses the penny in the square and shares a time a person might feel that way as well as a positive thought or helpful way to deal with that feeling. The penny toss counts if the majority of the penny is in the square - it is acceptable for the penny to be touching lines or to be partially in other squares. If the penny lands on no square however, the student looses that turn. The group may choose to keep tally of each person's points on the chart paper however stress that all students are winners if they handle their feelings in a positive way.*

4. **Closure:** Allow each student to take their penny with them to remind them, "a penny for a positive thought – it's worth it!"

Penny For Your Thoughts Game Sheet

Directions: As instructed in Procedure Step 3, write a feeling word and a point value from 5-15 in each square below and follow the directions given to play the game.

ACTIVITY D3.2
Shield of Self-Confidence

Purpose: To strengthen students' self-confidence.

Materials Needed:
- An armor shield – either a plastic toy shield or create a shield from poster board.
- Copy for each student of the Shield of Self-confidence Activity sheet
- Pencils

Procedures:
1. **Introduction:** Display an armor shield. Ask the students the purpose of a shield. Summarize that a shield was used for protection. In the days of the knights when they went into battle they were decked in their armor carrying a shield to protect their body from the arrows. Today we do not have the typical arrows coming at us to hurt us but there are problems and situations that come up that hurt our feelings. Allow students to brainstorm negative things that may happen to us that hurt our feelings. Include such situations as: being left out, trouble learning something new, getting laughed at, losing a game, etc. Tell the students that today we need a different kind of protection from the things that hurt us, we need our shield of self- confidence. Ask the students to define self-confidence. Summarize that self-confidence means the belief in yourself and your ability. Stress the importance of believing in yourself in order to handle life's problems.

2. Ask students: *Since self-confidence seems to be very important, where do we get self-confidence from?* Summarize that there may be times that people compliment us and we feel good about ourselves. However, the main building of our self-confidence needs to come from ourselves. We need to be the one appreciating when we do well and recognizing our own abilities. Each and everyday we need to look at our strengths and be proud. Hand each student a Shield of Self-Confidence Activity sheet to complete. The activity focuses on strengthening their self-confidence through each person appreciating what they do well, their positive qualities and things they do that they feel proud about. Allow students to share their completed shield of self-confidence.

3. Explain to students that now that they have their self-confidence information down on paper they need to get it in their head. Ask students to take a "pretend" permanent magic marker and to "pretend" to write the information from the shield onto their brain. Instruct students to keep their "pretend" magic marker and continue to add good information to their self-confidence shield in their brain. Pretend to hand students a "pretend" eraser to erase or get rid of any self doubts or negative thoughts that make it into the brain.

4. **Closure:** Encourage students to daily strengthen their self-confidence shield by taking time to appreciate what they did well that day.

Shield of Self-Confidence Activity Sheet

Directions: Complete the following.

1. Three things I do well...

_____

_____

_____

2. Three positive characteristics I have...

_____

_____

_____

1. Something I have done recently that I am proud of...

_____

_____

_____

_____

ACTIVITY D3.3
Love Notes

Purpose: To help students appreciate themselves.

Materials Needed:
• Copy for each student of the Love Notes Activity Sheet
• Chart paper and markers
• Pencils

Procedures:

1. **Introduction:** Ask: *Why do people write letters to others?* (to communicate) *What is a love note?* (a note written expressing positive feelings for someone). Explain to the group that we are going to write "love notes" today – a love note to ourselves.

2. On chart paper write different paragraph starter sentences. As a group you may want to create your own paragraph starters and/or use the following:
   • I like you because…
   • You are good at…
   • You help others by…
   To encourage a well written letter review the rules of paragraph writing. Remind them to begin with a topic sentence, write several detail sentences, and then a summary sentence before moving to the next paragraph. Hand each student a copy of Love Notes Activity sheet and allow time for them to write their letter.

3. Collect their letters. Keep the letters for two weeks and then send them to the students.

4. **Closure:** Encourage students to always appreciate and love themselves

Love Notes Activity Sheet

Dear Self,

_____

_____

_____

_____

_____

_____

_____

_____

_____

_____

Love,

ACTIVITY D3.4
Courage

Purpose: To help students develop their courage to face difficult situations.

Materials Needed:
- Copy and cut apart the letters to the newspaper on the Courage Activity sheet
- Pencils

Procedures:
1. **Introduction:** Ask: *What does courage means?* Share that courage is the ability to do something we are afraid of such as facing the unknown, dealing with hardship, or meeting challenges. All through life we will come across new situations for us that may be hard to face and handle or that we may be unsure of but it is important to develop the courage to make good choices and to face what we need to.

2. Ask: What are some situations when courage may be needed? Include such answers as: the first day of school, changing schools, moving, talking to an adult, and telling the truth in a difficult situation.

3. Hand to each group member a situation from the Courage Activity sheet. Share with the group that students have written to the newspaper's advice column for help and that you need their suggestions as to what advice to share. Allow students to share their answers encouraging other group members to add suggestions for each situation.

4. **Closure:** Remind students that courage takes a smile and an "I CAN" attitude.

Courage Activity Sheet

Directions: Copy and cut apart each letter to the newspaper's advice column. Ask students to give their advice and suggestions on how to use their courage to handle the situation.

Dear Wise Guy,

My family has just moved here from a different state. It is my first day of school as a new student at a school that I don't know anyone or anything. I'm scared. What should I do?

Signed,
I have the blues because I'm new

Dear Wise Guy,
On Wednesday our book reports are due. For this book report we have to stand up in front of the class and tell about our book. I'm worried that my mind will go blank and I won't know what to say and then I'll get embarrassed. What should I do?

Signed,
Speechless

Dear Wise Guy,
A kid in my school keeps bullying me – it scares me. What should I do?

Signed,
Scared stiff

Dear Wise Guy,

I don't like Math because it's too hard. When it's homework time I always have trouble with my math homework and I feel like giving up. What should I do?

Signed,
All figured out

Dear Wise Guy,

I accidentally broke the flower vase in our den at home when I was throwing a ball in the house. I didn't mean to – I was just throwing it up and down but then it slipped... I cleaned up all the broken pieces so mom and dad wouldn't know. The problem is that I feel guilty and should probably tell mom and dad what happened but I'm scared and don't know what to say. What should I do?

Signed,
Fumbled

Dear Wise Guy,

My friends I usually hang around with don't like the new kid but I do. I'm scared that if I go over to talk with the new student my friends will make fun of me and not like me anymore. What should I do?

Signed,
Peer pressured

271

POST ASSESSMENT ACTIVITY D
Pieces of the Puzzle

Purpose: To emphasize the importance of strengthening and maintaining a positive self-concept and to summarize the skills discussed in group.

Materials Needed:
- Copy of the Pieces of the Puzzle Activity Sheet for each student
- Pencils, pens, scissors
- Small plastic bags for each student
- Student Post Assessment Form copied for each student
- Parent/Teacher Assessment Form copied for each student
- Chart paper and marker

Procedures:

1. **Introduction:** Ask: *Have you ever worked on putting a puzzle together and come up with one puzzle piece short? What do you think or feel about the unfinished puzzle.* Summarize that the picture is just not quite right – it is incomplete. Relate to them that there are many pieces to our own puzzle – our puzzle of being lovable and capable and that it takes all the different pieces put together right to feel right.

2. Review with them the opening lesson of the different pieces of the "I Am Lovable and Capable" repair kit. Remind students that feeling lovable and capable does not come from outside events, getting things we like and things going our way, but it comes from inside you and how you choose to handle both the good and bad life has to offer. Write the different needed parts to being lovable and capable on chart paper that you have talked about in group. You may include such information as: knowing and appreciating my strengths, maintaining a positive thought even when things aren't perfect, maintaining a positive thought even when things are hard or difficult to do, maintaining a positive thought even when others may criticize or tease me, maintaining a positive thought even when I make a mistake and things do not go quite right, managing my feelings in a positive way, building on my strengths, and having the courage to speak up for myself and to try new things.

3. Hand each student an IALAC puzzle to complete. Instruct the students to choose all or some of the IALAC statements that they consider important to maintain a positive self image. Have them count the number of IALAC statements they want to add and then draw that number of puzzle shape pieces inside their IALAC sign. After the puzzle shapes have been drawn then students are to write the IALAC statement in each puzzle piece. Encourage them to add more information and strategy tips in each puzzle piece.

continued

4. When they have completed writing the information in the IALAC puzzle then instruct the students to cut apart the puzzle along the lines they drew. Allow students time to put their own puzzle together. Challenge them to use each of these puzzle pieces in life to help them strengthen and maintain a positive self-concept. Point out to students to be careful not to leave out one of their puzzle pieces because all are needed to make the picture complete. Give each student a plastic bag to put their puzzle pieces inside to take with them.

5. Ask students to complete the Student Post Assessment Form. Allow students to share information from their forms if they choose. Send out and collect the Parent/Teacher Post Assessment.

6. Celebrate the group, the time together, what you like about everyone, and point out their successes and improvements. Encourage others to do the same.

7. **Closure:** Challenge students to use the information on their IALAC puzzle in order to maintain a positive self-concept and to handle in a positive way the good and bad life has to offer.

Follow-up: Follow up with students individually, consulting with their teachers, and/or sending notes to the students to encourage and compliment. Consider scheduling a monthly support group.

Pieces of the Puzzle Activity Sheet

Directions: Copy the following for students to use to create their IALAC puzzle as instructed in Procedure Step 2. If possible, copy on heavy paper to create a better puzzle like piece.

Student Post Assessment For Self-Concept

Name: _____

Directions: Complete the following post assessment reflecting your present self-concept skills. Mark your answers honestly.

	STRONGLY AGREE	AGREE	DISAGREE	STRONGLY DISAGREE
1. I know and appreciate the good things about me and the things I can do well.	4	3	2	1
2. I can handle it even if things are not perfect.	4	3	2	1
3. I can think positively even if things are difficult or hard.	4	3	2	1
4. I can think positively even if I get criticized or teased by others.	4	3	2	1
5. I can think positively even if I make a mistake or things don't go quite right.	4	3	2	1
6. I have the skills to manage my feelings in a positive way.	4	3	2	1
7. I have the skills to build on my strengths to maintain a strong self-image.	4	3	2	1
8. I have the skills to speak up for myself and the courage to try new things.	4	3	2	1

9. What I enjoyed most about the group was: _____

_____

10. One thing I would recommend to change about group is _____

_____

Dear Parent/Teacher,

We are concluding our small group on self-concept that your child has been a participant. We have focused on the skills of:

I have enjoyed working with your child and will continue to follow up with your child during the year. To help assess the degree to which your child is implementing the skills learned, please complete the post assessment listed below and return. Your answers need to reflect your child's present behavior. Thank you.

Sincerely,

Your Child's Counselor

PARENT/TEACHER NEEDS ASSESSMENT FOR

STUDENT/CHILD'S NAME _____

	STRONGLY AGREE	AGREE	DISAGREE	STRONGLY DISAGREE
1. He/she knows and appreciates the good things about himself/herself and the things he/she can do well.	4	3	2	1
2. He/she can handle it even if things are not perfect.	4	3	2	1
3. He/she can think positively even if things are difficult or hard.	4	3	2	1
4. He/she can think positively even if he/she gets criticized or teased by others.	4	3	2	1
5 . He/she can think positively even if he/she makes a mistake or things don't go quite right.	4	3	2	1
6. He/she has the skills to manage his/her feelings in a positive way.	4	3	2	1
7. He/she has the skills to build on his/her strengths to maintain a strong self-image.	4	3	2	1
8. He/she has the skills to speak up for himself/herself and the courage to try new things.	4	3	2	1

Comments:

276

Service Learning

Service Learning
IN SMALL GROUP COUNSELING

WHAT?

Service Learning assignments are an additional component added to the small group counseling meetings in which students are given assignments in helping others in their school, family, and/or community. To encourage interest, involvement, and commitment to the service learning assignments, group members are invited to become members of the "Secret Service". Being a member of the Secret Service involves receiving weekly assignments in helping/serving others in which they are to perform during the week and report back the results at future meetings. Examples of assignments include: sending a compliment note to a classmate, helping the teacher clean up the room, doing something nice for a brother or sister, sending a thank you note to a helping adult at school, or picking up trash around the school.

WHY?

The purpose of adding a Service Learning Component to small group counseling is to provide group members with an opportunity to help others. The benefit for helping others has multiple positive effects. Not only does the recipient of the good deed feel positive but the doer of the good deed feels the benefit of having done something nice for someone else. The focus can move from ourselves and our wants and needs to focus on the needs of others. For example:

- For students working on anger issues, service learning helps them to focus on others, their needs and wants and replaces the self- focus with positive feelings of helping others.
- For students working on friendship skills, service learning gives them the opportunity to do nice things for others and to experience the positive feeling that comes from having been sensitive to others' needs.
- For students working on self- concept, service learning builds the positive feelings of self worth and importance in serving and doing for others.

The Service Learning Component also adds the opportunity to teach our students to become life long helpers. Taking the time to care about others and their needs is an important part of the success of any community and the happiness of individuals.

HOW?

In adding the service learning component to your group meetings, first allow for about 10 minutes at the initial meeting to introduce the concept to group members. (See the Secret Service Initial Information for Students for more information) Ask if they are interested in being a member of the Secret Service, to receive assignments each week in helping others, and to give a report at future meetings. If they choose/want/agree to be a member of the Secret Service then review the materials to select the assignment each week for the students. Make copies of the assignment for each student. Read over the assignment and discuss the "how" of the assignment so that each student understands. Emphasize the fun of secrecy as they follow through with the assignment. Point out the section on the assignment sheet for them to record the date of completion along with any notes on the assignment. Explain that they may include such information in their notes as: *How did it go?; What do you think the recipient of the good deed thought or felt?; What do you think or feel about doing the good deed?* In future group meetings allow about 5 minutes at the beginning of the group for students to report on their assignment and about 5 minutes at the end of the meeting to obtain a new Service Assignment for the coming week.

* Concept adapted from Mayes, S. (1996), Secret Agents. Pennsylvannia: Mar*co.

Secret Service
INITIAL INFORMATION FOR STUDENTS

PURPOSE: To introduce to the students the responsibilities of being a member of the school's secret service in which members receive assignments of helping others at school, at home and in the community.

PROCEDURE:

1. Ask students to name jobs in our community that help or serve others. Include such jobs as: nurse, doctor, teacher, fireman, police officer, minister … the list is endless.

2. Ask students to name jobs that people in our community volunteer their time to do in order to help others. Include such jobs as: volunteer firefighter, candy striper at the hospital, volunteer at the Red Cross, volunteer with church projects to help others in the community, volunteers at a food bank center, etc.

3. Ask students: *Why do you think people volunteer their time to help others?* (because people care about others and want to help out, perhaps someone in their lives helped them at a difficult time and they want to repay the favor.)

4. Ask: *What have you seen people doing for others at this school or in your neighborhood? What do you think people feel or think when someone does something nice for them? What do you think the person doing the good deed may think or feel about having done that good deed?*

5. Ask: *Have you ever heard of our country's Secret Service before? What is their job?* Explain the job as men and women who serve our country by protecting our leaders. They quietly perform their job making sure the person they are assigned to comes to no harm. Share with the students that they have the opportunity be a member of a similar secret service at our school. Explain that our school's Secret Service quietly does services helping others. Members of our school's secret service are given assignments to help others and then to report back the results/reaction of that good deed. Refer to the Requirements for Secret Service Membership on the next page and review this information with the students. Gain their support and willingness to be a part of the school's secret service performing good deeds.

   If your group is in agreement with serving on the school's Secret Service, you may choose to have them take a pledge to become a member. See the pledge given. Membership cards can also be copied and given to students who have taken the pledge and are members of your school's Secret Service. After students have chosen to be a part of the Secret Service, then you need to review the service assignments that are provided and choose an assignment for each week. Make copies of the assignment for each student. Allow about five minutes at the end of each group meeting to hand out and explain the "how to's" of the assignment. If time permits and the assignment involves a card or note, allow group time and materials for them to begin/or complete. On the assignment sheet review the area they can report about their good deed. Ask them to include how they think the other person may think or feel as well as how they think and feel about doing the good deed. Allow 5 minutes at the beginning of the next group meeting for students to report on their service assignment. You may choose to give a gold star sticker or some other simple reward for returning their completed assignment sheet.

REQUIREMENTS FOR MEMBERSHIP
IN THE
SCHOOL'S SECRET SERVICE

1. Have a willingness to help others. Care about others and want to be of service.

2. Follow through with the service assignment of the week and complete the assigned task to the best of your ability.

3. Whenever possible, you need to maintain the secrecy of the good deed.

4. Complete the report section on the sheet recording the reaction and results of the good deed and report this information to the group.

Secret Service Pledge

Say: *Raise your right hand and repeat after me.*

I, (state your name), do hereby pledge to serve and help others. As a member of the

_____ *'s Secret Service Team I will do good deeds and acts of kindness*

SCHOOL'S NAME

for others. I will follow through with assignments given and commit myself to caring and helping

others.

SECRET SERVICE MEMBERSHIP CARD

_____

is a member of the

_____'s Secret Service Team

(SCHOOL'S NAME)

committed to helping and doing good deeds for others.

_____   _____
(DATE)   (LEADER'S SIGNATURE)

Service Assignment:

Send a compliment note to a classmate telling something they do well. Make sure to send the note anonymously.

I will send a note to _____

About_____

Your Report:

Date Completed: _____

(How did it go? What do you think they thought or felt about the good deed? What did you think or feel about having done the good deed?)

_____

_____

_____

_____

_____

_____

_____

Submitted by,

_____

Service Assignment:

Find a student who seems to be alone at recess and offer to be his/her friend. Continue to talk with that person and show your friendliness.

Your Report:

Date Completed: _____

(How did it go? What do you think they thought or felt about the good deed? What did you think or feel about having done the good deed?)

_____

_____

_____

_____

_____

_____

_____

Submitted by,

_____

Service Assignment:

Say one nice thing to someone each day. Record your comment in the report.

Your Report: Date Completed: _____

(How did it go? What do you think they thought or felt about the good deed? What did you think or feel about having done the good deed?)

Monday: _____

Tuesday: _____

Wednesday: _____

Thursday: _____

Friday: _____

Saturday: _____

Sunday: _____

Submitted by,

_____

Service Assignment:

Write and send a thank you note to your parent.

I will send a note to _____

I will thank him/her for _____

_____

Your Report: Date Completed: _____

(How did it go? What do you think they thought or felt about the good deed? What did you think or feel about having done the good deed?)

_____

_____

_____

_____

_____

_____

_____

Submitted by,

_____

Service Assignment:

Do an extra chore around the house to help out your parents.

I plan to _____

Your Report: Date Completed: _____

(How did it go? What do you think they thought or felt about the good deed? What did you think or feel about having done the good deed?)

_____

_____

_____

_____

_____

_____

_____

Submitted by,

_____

Service Assignment:

Send your grandparents, aunt, uncle, or another adult friend a "thinking of you" card.

I will send a note to _____

_____

Your Report: Date Completed: _____

(How did it go? What do you think they thought or felt about the good deed? What did you think or feel about having done the good deed?)

_____

_____

_____

_____

_____

_____

_____

Submitted by,

_____

Service Assignment:

Pick up trash around the school — at recess, in the hallways, and in the classroom.

Your Report:

Date Completed: _____

(How did it go? What do you think they thought or felt about the good deed? What did you think or feel about having done the good deed?)

_____

_____

_____

_____

_____

_____

_____

Submitted by,

_____

Service Assignment:

Get together with a friend and with the permission of your parent, pick up trash in your yard and neighborhood.

Your Report:

Date Completed: _____

(How did it go? What do you think they thought or felt about the good deed? What did you think or feel about having done the good deed?)

_____

_____

_____

_____

_____

_____

_____

Submitted by,

_____

Service Assignment:

Do something extra nice for a brother or sister.

I will _____

Your Report:

Date Completed: _____

(How did it go? What do you think they thought or felt about the good deed? What did you think or feel about having done the good deed?)

_____

_____

_____

_____

_____

_____

_____

Submitted by,

_____

Service Assignment:

Write a thank you note to your teacher.

I will thank my teacher for _____

_____

_____

Your Report: Date Completed: _____

(How did it go? What do you think they thought or felt about the good deed? What did you think or feel about having done the good deed?)

_____

_____

_____

_____

_____

_____

_____

_____

Submitted by,

_____

Service Assignment:

Write a thank you note to an adult in your school – the principal, custodian, librian, etc.

I will write a thank you note to _____

I will thank them for _____

_____

Your Report: Date Completed: _____

(How did it go? What do you think they thought or felt about the good deed? What did you think or feel about having done the good deed?)

_____

_____

_____

_____

_____

_____

_____

Submitted by,

Service Assignment:

At lunch during the week, thank a cafeteria helper for fixing the lunches for the students.

I will say _____

_____

Your Report: Date Completed: _____

(How did it go? What do you think they thought or felt about the good deed? What did you think or feel about having done the good deed?)

_____

_____

_____

_____

_____

_____

_____

Submitted by,

_____

Service Assignment:

Thank a different adult at school, home, or in the community every day of the week. Record this information in your report.

Your Report:

Date Completed: _____

(How did it go? What do you think they thought or felt about the good deed? What did you think or feel about having done the good deed?)

Monday: _____

Tuesday: _____

Wednesday: _____

Thursday: _____

Friday: _____

Saturday: _____

Sunday: _____

Submitted by,

_____

Service Assignment:

Write a "Have a Happy Day" card to send to a local nursing home. Get as many students in your class to sign the card. Ask an adult to help you select a nursing home, find the address, and send the card.

_____

Your Report:

Date Completed: _____

(How did it go? What do you think they thought or felt about the good deed? What did you think or feel about having done the good deed?)

_____

_____

_____

_____

_____

_____

_____

Submitted by,

_____

Service Assignment:

During the week, do a kind deed for someone. You could help carry a teacher's book, clean up in your classroom without being asked to do so, help a friend, etc.

I will help by _____

_____

Your Report:

Date Completed: _____

(How did it go? What do you think they thought or felt about the good deed? What did you think or feel about having done the good deed?)

_____

_____

_____

_____

_____

_____

_____

Submitted by,

_____

Service Assignment: (Create your own service assignment)

Your Report: Date Completed: _____

(How did it go? What do you think they thought or felt about the good deed? What did you think or feel about having done the good deed?)

_____

_____

_____

_____

_____

_____

_____

Submitted by,

_____